ROOF TILING AND SLATING

A PRACTICAL GUIDE

ROOF TILING AND SLATING

A PRACTICAL GUIDE

KEVIN TAYLOR

THE CROWOOD PRESS

First published in 2008 by
The Crowood Press Ltd
Ramsbury, Marlborough
Wiltshire SN8 2HR

www.crowood.com

British Library Cataloguing-in-Publication Data
A catalogue record for this book is available from the British Library.

ISBN 978 1 84797 023 7

Dedication
This book is dedicated to all the great people in the roofing industry whom I have met over
the years, but especially to my father Alan, sadly no longer with us.

Disclaimer
The author and publisher do not accept responsibility, or liability, in any manner whatsoever
for any error or omission, nor any loss, damage, injury, or adverse outcome of any kind
incurred as a result of the use of any of the information contained in this book, or reliance
upon it. Readers are advised to obtain expert health and safety advice and specific professional
advice relating to their particular house, dwelling, project and circumstances before embarking
on any roofing, slating, tiling or building work of any kind.

Typeset by Jean Cussons Typesetting, Diss, Norfolk
Printed and bound in Malaysia by Times Offset (M) Sdn Bhd

Contents

Preface and Acknowledgements

I left school not knowing what I wanted to do for a living and so I decided to work for my father's roofing company, for what I thought would be a few weeks until I found what I considered to be a proper job. Twenty-five years on and counting I am still in the roofing industry, despite several half-hearted attempts to leave it; it is, as they say, 'in the blood'.

I hope that, as well as providing actual guidance on slating and tiling, this book will help in some way to encourage more people into what is still a cracking little trade; yes, it is hard work and you have the weather in the winter to contend with, but the freedom, the variety, the sense of pride on seeing the finished roof (something which lasts for years as you drive by places with which you have been involved), the banter on site, and the useful money you can now earn more than make up for the drawbacks.

It is true to say that roofers have not always enjoyed the best of reputations, but I have to say that, in my experience, most of the 'cowboy' roofer stories involve people who are not really roofers at all. If more homeowners went to reputable firms rather than the 'unmarked van and mobile phone-only brigade' then they would see that most do a good job at a fair price.

Roofing in general is full of people who are knowledgeable, skilful, passionate, cynical, funny, opinionated, resourceful and argumentative, but rarely dull. Many of them – depending on their age, regional differences or personal grudges – may read this book and no doubt disagree with some of it, but I have not tried to write a technically perfect manual that covers every eventuality. Instead, I have tried to write a book that covers commonly used methods, which are simple to understand and to follow.

Most of the photographs here were taken in a workshop situation on training rigs rather than on site. This allowed me to set up the exact situations I wanted, so I would like to thank the staff at Sandtoft Training and Assessment Centre (STAC) in Doncaster for allowing me to use their facilities.

Introduction

Slating and tiling embraces a vast area of materials and situations, from re-tiling a front door porch to the restoration of a cathedral and everything in between. To cover all of these crafts and techniques and to make the text appropriate for the many types of person who potentially make up its readership could take many volumes to complete. Thus to cover the basics has proved quite difficult to do within one book of manageable size, but you will find that most of the common skills required in roof slating and tiling are covered in chapter 6, dealing with interlocking tiles, since these are by far the most frequently used material. To get the most out of the book you should read it as it has been printed, at least until the end of chapter 6.

This book is aimed at serious DIYers, self-builders, students, improvers and those new to the trade, but it may also prove useful for more experienced roofers. It covers the tools, techniques and tips needed to install common materials, interlocking and plain tiles, natural and artificial slates on small to medium-sized projects with standard roof shapes and details. The book provides easy-to-follow instructions and techniques, tips on what to do (and what to avoid) and, above all, guidance on good practice. Its purpose is to help the reader to achieve a good quality roof, which will be durable, looks professional and, above all, keeps the water out.

While I have tried to ensure that the methods are in line with all the current British Standards (BS) and Health and Safety requirements, the book is not meant to be a substitute for them. Had I done so, it would have turned into a very long, vague, highly technical and possibly very dull piece of work, full of ifs, buts and maybes. Professional roofers and those who are intending to work on commercial projects should refer to the following publications as a minimum:

> BS 5534:2003, Code of practice for slating and tiling (including shingles)
> BS 8000, Workmanship on building sites Part 6: 1990 Code of practice for slating and tiling of roofs and claddings (under revision at the time of writing)
> Health and Safety in Roof Work – Health and Safety Guidance 33 (HSG33)

The first two are produced by the British Standards Institute and the third by the Health and Safety Executive. If you are intending to do your own lead work in a commercial environment I would also recommend a fourth publication – the *Lead Sheet Manual* produced by the Lead Sheet Association (LSA). I have provided details on how to get all these publications in the contacts list at the back of the book.

THE FUNCTION AND PURPOSE OF SLATING AND TILING

The main function of slating and tiling is, of course, to keep the building watertight, to give it a good hat if you like. But slating and tiling are about much more than that, they are highly visual parts of a building, which add to the character of our townscapes in every aspect, from domestic dwellings to buildings of high historical importance.

One side effect of reading this book, I hope, is that you will feel compelled to look up at roofs and to comment on them in your daily life and wherever you go. Those of us in roofing will recognize this affliction (and so, I suspect, would our partners). If you travel about this country extensively you start to notice the character that roofing materials add to places. For example, the clay pantile roofs in areas such as Norfolk and Lincolnshire, the stone slates in the Yorkshire Dales, the different types of natural slate found in Wales, Scotland and the South-West, and the clay plain tiles that give so much character to many of our older domestic properties. Sometimes these materials are deemed to be so important to a building that they are relaid wherever possible, a process that I and other supporters of our heritage just love to see.

While much of what we do has not changed perhaps for hundreds of years, there is another side to roof slating and tiling and that is the new materials and techniques that have emerged and continue to do so. Concrete interlocking tiles and artificial slates have provided a cost-effective range available in a variety of finishes and colours for the new build and refurbishment market, we have modern roof windows which are relatively easy to install, dry-fix systems that replace sand/cement mortar with plastic alternatives, and high-tech roofing felts (underlay) that can 'breathe' to help to combat condensation. These new materials are also shaping our townscapes and have added enormously to the 'pallet' of roofing materials that can now be offered by the roofing industry.

DESIGN CONSIDERATIONS

What roofing materials you use depends on how much you want to spend, how you want the roof to look and, in many cases, what the local authority will allow you to do.

Cost

With regards to cost, it is not just the price per tile or slate that matters, it is how long it will take to lay it and the other materials that go with it. In general, concrete, interlocking, tiled roofs are at the cheaper end, with clay plain tiles and natural slates being the most expensive. Somewhere in the middle are concrete plain tiles, artificial slates and a range of interlocking and traditional clay roof tiles. All the roofing materials sold by reputable merchants and manufacturers in the United Kingdom have to pass stringent tests so all should provide you with a sound weatherproof covering; provided, of course, that they are fixed properly.

Quality

What you will pay extra for is mainly to do with aesthetics and long-term durability. A good quality slate or clay tile, for example – apart from perhaps darkening – will change little in appearance throughout its useful life and can normally be reused (hence there is also an environmental recycling factor with some materials). Cheaper materials tend to become discoloured and hosts for moss, lichen and other plant growths, some within just a few years of being laid and are rarely, if ever, reused. However, some roof-tile manufacturers do have the facility to recycle old tiles.

Planning Issues

If you are re-roofing then the first thing you need to do is to approach your local authority and ask to speak to the planning department and building control. There are three important reasons why you should do this.

Restrictions

The first is that your property may be in a conservation area or there may be restrictions on the range of materials you can use for aesthetic reasons. This does not necessarily mean that the property has to be hundreds of years old or be listed, it may well be that local authority policy is to retain a certain look to the buildings in a particular area.

Structural Issues

The second is that the roof structure may need to be inspected and approved to ensure that it is of an adequate strength and condition to be re-roofed with the new materials, especially, of course, if there is a suspicion that the new materials will be heavier than the existing ones.

Conservation of Heat and Power

The third concerns a recent change in the Building Regulations in relation to the conservation of heat and power (Approved Document Part L). If you are replacing more than 25 per cent of a roof then it is very likely that you will be required to upgrade your insulation as well. Of the three reasons, this is the most current and the one most likely to have an adverse effect on you later on if you ignore it. The local authority can insist that the work is done (often more awkward or expensive later on) and you may experience problems selling the property until it has been carried out.

HEALTH AND SAFETY

Working at Height

Working at heights requires special precautions for obvious reasons. Falls from height still account for one-fifth of the deaths in the construction industry; they are the biggest killer in the industry, yet still people chance their arm, especially in the domestic market. Having seen one former colleague suffer an accident that meant that he could never walk again, another break his leg and countless near misses, I can tell you that it is just not worth risking your neck to save money or to win contracts. People often say that health and safety are expensive, but there is a saying to the effect that 'if you think health and safety are expensive then you should try accidents', and in our litigious world it was never truer. Approximately 8.5 per cent (about £4.75bn) of tender prices are lost due to deaths and injuries and the resulting claims and court actions in the construction industry.

For any short-term work (less than an hour) the minimum safety equipment required on a pitched roof is an access ladder plus a roof ladder. However, if you have good edge protection and you can use the battens (which must be in good condition) as footholds, then normally you do not necessarily need a roof ladder.

For anything more extensive than a few roof repairs you should have a suitable working platform. This can be anything from a lightweight, quick-form tower (from a hire shop) to a full tube and fitting scaffold. The choice is based on the risks involved, but certainly for full new or re-roofs you should

employ a competent scaffolder to erect a scaffold fit for purpose. The working platform should be as close to the eaves as possible (set no more than 300mm down), because you should be able to step safely on and off the roof without any risk of injury.

You should also ensure that, if there is any chance that you could fall through a roof (that is, between the rafters), you should consider the risks and put the correct controls in place. Internal protection can range from boarding out above the ceiling joists, to air bags and full safety netting on larger projects.

The following checklists should help with regard to providing a safer working environment while carrying out roofing work:

Access ladders must:
- be set at an angle of 75 degrees (a ratio of one out, four up);
- securely lashed or clamped (preferably at the top) or footed by another person;
- extend at least 1m or five rungs over the step-off point;
- be climbed and descended by using at least three points of contact (that is, two feet and at least one hand).

Roof ladders must:
- be of sufficient length to reach the access ladder;
- be factory-made to recognized quality standards, not hand-made from timber;
- be lashed to the access ladder close to the step-off point.

Working platforms must:
- be fully boarded and close to the eaves;
- have a handrail at 950mm or more up from the working platform;
- have an intermediate safety rail between the working platform and the handrail;
- have toe-boards with a minimum height of 150mm;
- be fitted with brick guards or similar, especially when stripping roofs.

Personal Protective Equipment (PPE)

Personal protective equipment is the last resort in

A selection of personal protective equipment used by roofers (clockwise from the top: hard toe-capped boots, heavy-duty gloves, high-impact goggles, disposable dust mask, ear defenders and hard hat).

health and safety. This means that, if you have to put yourself at risk to do the work because there is no other way of designing out the hazards, then you need to wear the right equipment. The standard PPE for a roofer would include a pair of heavy-duty gloves to wear when loading the tiles or slates, appropriate protective footwear, a hard hat and, when mixing or using a disc cutter, eye protection, ear defenders and dust masks. When choosing PPE you should always ensure that the items are fit for purpose, especially eye protection, which should be selected to cope with any impact force that may be placed on it. If in doubt, then always buy from a reputable hire shop or DIY store and explain what you want the PPE for before buying it. But, whatever you do, do not just go for the cheapest, getting the right equipment could save you from a bad injury.

Lowering and Lifting Materials

Wherever possible, you should try to avoid carrying things up or down a ladder because of the risks involved with your falling or dropping something. Often, of course, on small projects and one-offs it is not practicable to hire or buy specialist equipment, but I shall briefly cover the main ones in use for those who may be intending to work in more commercial environments.

Forklift Truck

Virtually every site will now have a forklift truck to move, load and unload lorries and raise and lower materials. Only trained and designated people should operate the forklift. Materials raised to working-platform level should be placed on special loading bays designed to take their weight, not on the main scaffolding.

Vertical Cage Hoist

Cage hoists are normally used on buildings that are of three storeys or more and, in particular, where there are many pedestrians such as a town centre or in public buildings. They should be erected and dismantled by approved, competent people only, and the user must have undergone the correct training (often training is carried out on the job, by the hire company).

Inclined Hoist

The roofs on most one- and two-storey properties can be serviced by an inclined hoist. There is a range of these available, normally they are designed to take bricks and blocks as well as slates and tiles up to the working platform and they do this via a series of raised plates attached to a belt or chain driven by a fuel-powered generator at the bottom. Unlike a cage hoist, which is for others to erect and dismantle, most inclined hoists are set up, used and taken down by the roofer. When purchasing one of these hoists the companies often offer free training on how to do this safely.

Chute

When stripping a roof it is important to ensure that you use a chute or some other safe means of lowering the materials (for example, in a container by forklift truck). This is particularly important in areas where you would expect to find many pedestrians or on a public highway. Chutes should be erected and dismantled by a competent person, normally the same one who erected the scaffold.

Gin Wheel

For small loads that can be properly secured and pulled up by hand, gin wheels can prove an effective, low-cost item. Apart from the obvious point of not trying to lift or lower more weight than you are physically comfortable with, the important things to remember are that the gin wheel should be in good condition and correctly fixed to the scaffold, the rope must be also be in good condition, the area below cordoned off (just in case), the method of hooking and unhooking pre-established and the user wearing gloves.

MEASUREMENTS

Metric vs. Imperial

Many slaters and tilers still work in imperial measurements and some (like me) switch between imperial and metric to suit the situation. But, if you are new to the trade, I would encourage you to use metric only for two main reasons: first, because converting from one to the other can cause errors, and secondly, most things (including setting and marking out) are much easier to learn in metric. By now, of course, we should all be working in metric, and so, at the risk of upsetting some of my peers, I have (apart from the occasional reference to explain a point) tried to avoid imperial measurements throughout this book.

CHAPTER 1

Tools and Equipment

This chapter deals with the tools and equipment needed and advice on how to make the right choices.

HAND TOOLS

The tools in a roofer, slater and tiler's bag or tool box will vary from firm to firm and from region to region, and so will the terminology describing them. The list below is from my own tools and those which are most commonly used throughout the industry. Much, of course, depends on the type of work you are doing, so I have included a brief description of what each tool is used for to help you decide what you may or may not need.

Measuring Tape

Retractable tapes come in all sorts of quality and length, but for measuring roofs and for general use go for a heavy-duty, retractable tape in excess of 7m long.

Folding Rule

Many roofers (including me) prefer to use a folding rule rather than a tape in certain situations. Go for a 1m folding rule that shows metric and, if possible, imperial measurements as well.

Gauging Trowel

The trowel most commonly used by roofers is the gauging trowel (about 175mm in length). It is big enough to bed mortar with and small enough to point with. Go for a forged trowel, which means that the blade and the handle are all of one piece of metal; the cheaper ones are welded together and not really robust enough for roofing work.

Nail Pouch

There is a wide variety of nail pouches available, some are more tool belts than pouches and, while the odd extra pocket or loop is handy at times, a simple nail pouch with two separate compartments should be fine in most situations. This will allow you to separate batten nails and clout nails for 'lathing and felting' and then tile and slate nails and clips (if applicable) when fixing the roof covering.

Chalk Line/Wet Red Line

Lines are useful for striking lines when battening and setting out for tiling, for example. If you are using a wet line choose one that is quite stiff, absorbent (that is, not nylon) and well made. The sign of a good line is that it does not separate when twisted backwards and forwards in the fingers. The colouring used is normally red cement dye mixed with water. If you prefer a chalk line then buy a heavy duty one and fill it with a coloured chalk.

Trimming Knife

This is still commonly referred to in the trade as a 'Stanley knife', although that is strictly a trade name. They are used mainly for cutting underlay. Straight blades will cut most types of felt and underlay, but if you are using bituminous felt I would recommend hook blades.

Cordless Drill/Screwdriver

By all means have a manual drill and a few straight and cross-bladed screwdrivers in your tool bag as a backup and for small jobs, but, if you are going to be doing a lot of dry fix or installing roof windows, then

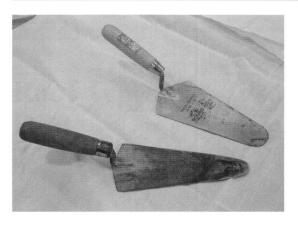

Roofers' gauging trowel.

Nail pouches.

Selection of slating tools (clockwise from the top: slate-holing machine, slate knife, slate ripper, break iron, pick hammer and hand-held cutters).

a cordless drill (the higher the voltage the better) plus a selection of masonry bits and screwdriver bits are essential.

Slater's 'Break or Bench' Iron and Slate Knife

A break iron is basically an anvil for cutting natural slates in conjunction with a slate knife. These are the traditional tools used to cut slates and are still widely used, despite the introduction of hand-held cutters, especially when it comes to the heavier, thicker slates.

Slate-Holing Machines

Now many natural slates come pre-holed, but you do pay a premium for that service and there are some occasions when it is preferable to hole the slates yourself. Slate-holing machines can have a punch- or borer-type action and come with adjustable guards to set the holing position. Traditionally, a slater's apprentice or labourer would set up a bench with a break iron, slate knife and holing machine and it would be his job to grade (into three or more thicknesses) and hole all the slates and cut the fittings (half slates, under-eaves, topper slates and so on) for the craftsman.

Slate Cutters (Hand-Held)

Used for cutting thin, natural slates and artificial, fibre-cement slates.

Claw Hammer or Lath Hammer

Which hammer to use for lathing and felting is a matter of personal preference. At one time, nearly all roofers used a lath hammer (the modern ones are actually plastering drywall hammers) because you were allowed to chop the battens rather than saw them, as happens now. For most roofers, it seems that a decent claw hammer is now the weapon of choice.

Pick Hammer

This is the traditional slater's hammer, with the pick being used for making holes in situ and the small head providing the accuracy needed to nail slates without breaking them.

Cross Pein Hammer

I have always carried one of these in my tool box

Cross pein (tiling) hammer.

since I was an apprentice because it is very handy for chipping away bits of tile, taking nibs off and for picking up and nailing roof tiles. I have not seen them often over the years so perhaps it is a local preference, but if you are doing much roof tiling then I would recommend that you get one; buy a decent make and go for one with some weight to it (say 250 to 300g).

Tile Nibbler

This tool is designed for cutting clay and concrete plain tiles (the blades are adjustable) without having to resort to power tools. The tile is marked and passed through the blades as they are worked up and down, taking off about 10 to 12mm at a time. For the best results the tile should be scribed first.

Tile Scribe

Scribes are useful when hand cutting because they give you a better chance of making the cut in the first place and the results are normally much neater. Go for one with a good handle that you can grip so that you can apply the appropriate pressure when scribing.

Basic Lead-Working Tools

As the name suggests, snips are used for cutting thin metal and in roofing that normally means sheet lead.

The dressers are used to beat the lead into place and the chisels for chasing out masonry joints and positioning the lead into the joints.

Saws

Since truss rafters became popular, it has been standard practice to saw battens rather than to chop them with a lath hammer. You should choose a fine-tooth saw or a bow saw, some roofers carry both.

Hand Board

Along with a suitable heavy-duty bucket, I would recommend the use of a hand board for applying mortar and especially when pointing.

RIGHT: Tile nibbler and scribes.

BELOW: Selection of leadwork tools (clockwise from the top: masonry chisels, bolster, snips and lead dressers).

Petrol-driven disc cutter.

Staple Gun

Since plastic underlays became popular, many roofers now prefer to use heavy-duty staple guns as an alternative to nailing.

Wrecking Bar

Also known as a crowbar, wrecking bars are useful tools if your work involves stripping roofs. They give you a lot more leverage than a claw hammer and can be especially useful when removing old battens and timbers.

Wood Chisel

This is handy for taking notches out of fascia boards and similar such jobs where small sections of timber need to be removed to assist in the laying of slates, tiles and components.

PLANT AND EQUIPMENT

Cement Mixers

For small amounts, it is common practice to mix mortar by hand, but, if you require more than a few bucketfuls, then you should consider using a mixer. Portable cement mixers are readily available from plant- and tool-hire shops. Portable mixers may be electric or petrol-driven (larger mixers are normally diesel-powered). Which one you choose depends largely on personal preference and obviously whether or not you have access to a power supply.

Disc Cutters

When you hire a disc cutter you will also need the correct type of blade, fuel and the necessary PPE (that is, goggles, ear defenders and dust masks). All of these should be available from a hire shop.

Ladders

When buying or hiring a ladder it is important to check that it is in good condition and is of the correct length for the job. When erected, the ladder should be at an angle of around 75 degrees to the ground with at least five rungs above the step-off point. Always make sure that the ladder is lashed at the top so that it cannot move. Heavy-duty aluminium extension ladders are perhaps the most versatile, but on most sites you will find that wooden pole ladders are still preferred.

Roof Ladders

Roof ladders, also known as roof crawlers or 'cat' ladders in some parts, should be used for minor repairs only or inspections. Anything more extensive than this will require a working platform. As with normal ladders, check that the roof ladder is in good condition and is of the right length for the job. Most roof ladders are made of aluminium and come with wheels so that they can be rolled up the roof and then flipped over into position. Make sure that the hook is firmly located behind the ridge and that the bottom of the roof ladder is lashed to the access ladder.

CHAPTER 2

Materials

This chapter describes the range of materials covered in this book and, at the same time, introduces the reader to more terminology. There will be general descriptions of some of the more popular proprietary systems available and advice on how and why you should obtain individual fixing guides from the manufacturers.

COMMON MATERIALS

Underlay

Felt

For many years the most common type of underlay used under slates and tiles was the bituminous felt Type 1F. This is still widely used in the domestic sector, but it has all but totally been replaced on new sites by a range of high-tech, plastic underlays. 1F felt typically comes in 1m by 15m rolls. Many roofers, and therefore merchants, will refer to all underlays as 'felt', irrespective of the actual type.

Plastic Underlays and Breather Membranes

Most modern underlays are made from some form of plastic and many of these are designed to be 'breather membranes'. These, incorporating thousands of micro-holes, are produced in rolls up to 50m in length and widths of 1 and 1.5m. The holes are designed to be small enough to prevent water droplets from coming through but large enough to let water vapour escape. All roofs need to be ventilated to prevent condensation and there has been much argument about whether or not breather membranes are sufficient to do this without additional

vents (known as non-vented systems). If you are considering using a non-vented system you should first consult its manufacturer and whoever is responsible for the roof design and specification.

Battens

Most reliable merchants should stock only roofing battens that are produced from Grade A softwood imported from Scandinavia. The most common sizes are 50mm × 25mm and 38mm × 25mm. The size you need depends on the rafter centres and the type of material you are using. If in doubt, use the larger size for all interlocking tiles and any types of slate, and the smaller size for plain tiles only. A third size, 38mm × 19mm, was used on old roofs for slates and plain tiles but is now no longer acceptable unless it is used on a fully boarded roof.

It should be noted that even battens that are marked as complying with current British Standards still require the user to make a final site check on them before they are used, a process known as grading. Typically, you should check for large knots, knots that have dropped out of the timber, splits, distortions and badly waned (that is, slanted or curved) edges. Note that moderately waned edges are not a problem provided that they are used correctly: they should be placed at the top edge for slates and the bottom edge for tiles and in both cases face the installer. Experienced roofers do check battens as they are working and will discard defective ones on the basis that they will cause problems later on when the slates or tiles have been fixed. Recently, fully graded battens have entered the market, which remove the need to grade on site, although you should expect to pay a premium for these products.

Nails

Batten Nails

The requirement of any nail or fixing is to transfer enough resistance to stand up to the forces placed on it and to prevent the attachment from coming off again. There are now a variety of nails in use, from standard, round-headed wire nails (normally galvanized) to improved (for instance, ribbed or helical) nails, some of which come in cartridges to be used with gas-powered nailing guns. Standard nails for 25mm-deep battens should be 65mm in length and at least 3.35mm in diameter.

Felt Nails and Tacks

Felt should be fixed with large-headed, clout nails at least 25mm in length and made of galvanized wire or aluminium. If you are using a plastic underlay you may wish to use a heavy-duty staple gun to fix it.

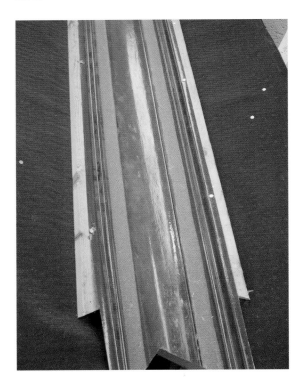

Slate and Tile Nails

It is important to check with the manufacturer or supplier that the nails are correct for the particular slate or tile you are working with. If the wrong nails are used and this contributes to tiles or slates coming off, then it is possible that the installer could be found negligent if a dispute occurred.

In general, most tile nails are aluminium alloy clouts, with their lengths and diameters varying depending on the profile and the depth of the tile or slate. Like batten nails, they may be standard or improved to give extra resistance. For natural slates and some artificial ones, copper clout nails starting at a minimum length of 30mm are normally specified.

Valley Liners

Unless you are going to use lead sheet in the valleys, the most common way to line valleys is now with a preformed, glass reinforced plastic (GRP) liner. The liners normally come in lengths of 2.4 to 3.0m and, if they are to be used for materials that require mortar bedding or pointing (for instance, interlocking tiles), will have sanded strips running parallel to the centre line. Conversely, valley liners without sanded strips are used with materials that do not require mortar bedding (such as slates).

Felt Support Trays

Felt support trays do two important jobs. The first is that they prevent the felt or underlay from sagging behind the fascia board and therefore prevent a trough from forming, which could gather water and, at some point, leak. The second is that they offer a non-perishable, leading edge into the gutter, meaning that the felt or underlay (most are not designed for open exposure) can be set back away from the sun's ultra-violet rays and other destructive elements.

Hip Irons

Hip irons are galvanized metal bars twisted into a scroll and with two or more holes in them for fixing to the roof. They are fixed to the hip rafter with two screws or nails to ensure that the hip tiles do not slide

Typical GRP valley liner.

Typical felt support trays.

off the roof as they are being fixed, and to offer long-lasting support once the mortar has set.

Undercloak

This is the name given to any material that provides an overhang at the verge on which to bed mortar. This could be natural or artificial slates, plain tiles or, now more commonly, fibre-cement strips. Slates that are normally cut into widths of 150mm or greater and plain tiles are laid face down so that the 'good' side can be seen when looking up from ground level. Fibre-cement strips normally come in lengths of 1.2 or 2.4m and in a variety of widths, the most common being 150mm. One side is smooth (the 'good' side) and the other has a dimpled effect like a golf ball to provide a better key for the verge mortar.

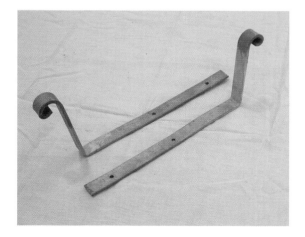

Hip irons.

19

Popular types of concrete-interlocking tile.

SLATES AND TILES

Concrete Interlocking Tiles

These are the most popular in Britain because they are relatively cheap, quick to lay and come in a range of colours, finishes (that is, smooth or granular) and profiles (shapes). The profiles shown here are among the most commonly found in Britain although it is important to note that each manufacturer's tiles will vary slightly so it is important not to mix them together. Each tile type will have a minimum pitch at which it can be laid under warranty, so it is important to check this before you place your order.

Plain Tiles

Plain tiles are the traditional, small, rectangular tiles still found on many old properties around Britain. Clay plain tiles have been available for hundreds of years and are still being produced today. Concrete plain tiles, which appeared much later, are readily available, come in a range of colours and finishes and are cheaper than their clay equivalents.

Standard fittings include under-eaves/tops tiles, which are needed to create a double course at the bottom and the top edge of a roof, and tile-and-a-half (sometimes referred to as gable tiles), which are used to create a half bond on every other course. There are also a number of fittings for plain tiling to hips, valleys and vertical areas.

Natural Slates (Regular-Sized, Centre-Nailed)

Slates native to Wales or Cumbria are still regarded by many as perhaps the best in the world, although they can be considerably more expensive than imported ones. The vast majority of slates now used in the United Kingdom are imported from Spain but also come from other countries such as China, Canada and Brazil. It is important to remember that slates are a natural product and may vary tremendously in quality from one quarry to another. In other words, you cannot tar all slates from one country with the same brush; with slates you normally get what you pay for, and so it is fair to say that price generally reflects quality.

Artificial Slates (Fibre-Cement)

Such a slate is easily identifiable by the neatly formed nail holes just above their centre and the single rivet hole near the tail. Because they are machine-made, there should be no variance in thickness and so it

Plain tiles and related fittings (clockwise from top left: bonnet hip, valley tile, left/right-handed vertical angles, eaves/tops tile, standard plain tile and tile-and-a-half).

takes less skill to lay them than natural slates. Wide slates (slate-and-a-half and doubles) are available for use at the verge, valley, hip ends and at abutments. A range of fittings including special verge units, hip and ridge tiles is also available.

Ridge/Hip Tiles

These are either part-round or angled and normally made from the same material as the roof covering (that is, clay or concrete). There are also ornamental ridge/hip tiles, which are normally made to order, along with highly ornate end tiles called finials. Ridge tiles and hip tiles are essentially the same, the only real difference being that those designed specifically for the hips are not as steep (that is, flatter, not as angled or round) as ridge tiles.

Dentil Slips

These are small, rectangular pieces of clay or concrete designed to be inserted into the pans (low points) of roof tiles, with a pan depth of 25mm or more when bedding hip or ridge tiles. The purpose of the dentil slip is to reduce the size of the mortar bed and thereby combat the shrinkage and cracking that can result. They also provide some degree of decoration to the ridge or hip detail.

MORTAR COMPONENTS

The Standard Mix

The mortar mix for roofing work should be a ratio of three parts sand to one part ordinary Portland cement (OPC). Where possible, you should use a

A selection of ridge/hip tiles (clockwise from top left: angle, segmental (part-round, crested and half-round).

coarse 'sharp sand', which contains a bigger range of particle size, rather than the softer 'building sand', since it provides a higher tensile strength on setting and is generally recognized as being more durable against weathering. Old roofs were normally done in sharp sand, and anyone who has tried to strip one will tell you how hard the stuff can set. However, some sharp sands can be difficult to mix correctly and produce mortar that is difficult to work with (especially on deeper beds) and, because of this, many prefer building sand as it tends to produce a smoother, more cohesive workable mix. Building sand will do if you cannot find good sharp sand that mixes well, although I would recommend that you should add at least some sharp sand to the mix.

Additives (Plasticizers and Colourings)

Plasticizers
These are additives that bind the water, sand and cement together better to produce a smoother, tackier and more workable mix. If you do not use plasticizers the water may rise to the top of the mix and there is a tendency for the mortar to slump more, be difficult to point up and the resulting set may be weak, with poor adhesive qualities. Plasticizers come in both liquid and powder form and should be used as directed.

Colourings
Like plasticizers, colourings come in liquid or powder

form and should be used as instructed. It is worth pointing out that, when the mortar is dry, it may be considerably paler than when in the wet state. This is mainly due to the bleaching effect of the cement and the sun, especially on south-facing elevations. An alternative to colourings is to use a coloured sand (such as black or red), which may be more expensive but is simpler and can be more consistent in quality purely because there is no measuring of dye to be done.

DRY FIX SYSTEMS

General

Dry fix systems are designed to attach a variety of components to a roof without the use of mortar. The manufacturers' argument for dry fix is that mortar is a weakness and an inconsistency that is best avoided where possible. Traditionalists, of course, will argue that there is nothing wrong with mortar if it is mixed properly and put on correctly, and I would strongly support this view. However, in the real world there is increasing evidence (especially on new work) that there are more mortar failures than there used to be, probably due to a combination of factors such as poor workmanship, the wrong type of

sand, the wrong mix (strength) and increased movement in modern roof construction. Dry fix is considerably more expensive than its mortar equivalent and aesthetically may not be to everyone's taste, but the systems are simple to fix and, provided that they are installed to the manufacturers' instructions, should be maintenance-free, and there is the added benefit that they will be under warranty.

In most cases the manufacturer of the roof tiles will offer a system specifically designed to go with them; alternatively, there is an increasing number of universal systems on the market.

Dry Ridge

There are three main types of dry ridge system currently available. One uses a continuous plastic rail, which also acts as the top batten, one uses shorter plastic rails that clip together and sit on top of the tiles or slates, and one uses an adhesive-backed, flexible roll (rapid type). All the systems use brackets known as 'unions', which sit in the joints between the ridge tiles. If you tell your supplier which type of tile or slate you are using and the total ridge length, he should be able to provide you with all the components you need, along with the fixing instructions and fixing kits.

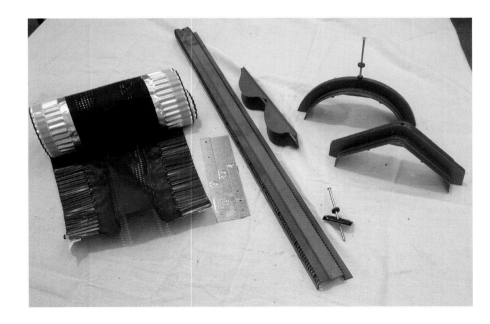

A selection of dry ridge components (left to right: ridge roll, ridge batten strap, ventilation strip, profile filler, unions, drive screw and sealing washer and plate).

A selection of dry verge components (left to right: slate verge rail, interlocking and cloaked verge).

Cloaked Verge

Cloaked verge tiles or slates are special fittings made to finish off the left- and the right-hand verge of the roof. These systems are relatively expensive, but they are considered by many to be aesthetically more pleasing than their plastic counterparts and are just about as quick and as simple to lay as normal tiles or slates. These are made only for certain products, so you will need to check their availability with your supplier or the manufacturer.

Interlocking Verge Units

These are individual plastic units that slide or snap together and tend to be mechanically fixed (that is, nailed) as well. They are normally designed for use with single-lap interlocking tiles. Depending on the tile being used, the verge units will be made by the same manufacturer or your merchant may be able to offer you a universal alternative.

Continuous Dry Verge 'Rails'

These tend to be for thinner materials such as artificial or natural slates. Again, there is a variety of systems available, which can be made product-specific or universal. Generally, rails are nailed to the ends of the battens, with the edges of the slates tucked into a section which returns back towards the roof.

Dry Hips

Dry hip systems are similar to dry ridge systems; in fact, some, such as the rapid adhesive roll types, are sold as ridge/hip systems. But there is more work involved with hips than with dry ridge because the slates or tiles that come into the hip all need to be cut and fixed in place, and, if an adhesive roll is to be used, then the cut slates or tiles need to be cleaned and dried to remove any dust, water or debris or there will be a chance that they will not stick properly.

Some roofs 'kick' at the eaves; this means that the tiles or slates on the bottom course tilt up, either because the fascia board is too high or the roof has been intentionally built to shallow out the lower courses (known as a sprocket). Some rigid systems will struggle to cope if the roof kicks at the eaves, so this is something to consider when you are asking questions about which one to use.

Dry Valleys

There are now several dry-valley systems available for more or less the full range of slates and tiles. Most dry valleys have a central ridge running along their full length and come in different heights for different roof coverings. Unlike traditional open valleys, the slates or tiles are cut tight to the sides of the central ridge with no visible gaps. As with all dry

fix, it is important to read the instructions carefully and to adhere to them to ensure that the details are correct and to comply with the requirements of the warranty.

WHERE TO BUY

DIY Superstores

Increasingly now, well-known DIY superstores are stocking more and more specialist products and can prove to be very handy for last-minute items and general materials. There will be sand, cement, timber battens and some of the more common materials aplenty, but the range and quantities of slates, tiles, fittings and fixings may be quite limited, as may be the advice and guidance that you need from time to time.

Typical dry hip system (left to right: hip roll, union, drive screw with sealing washer and plate, hip tray).

Typical dry valley system.

Many builders' merchants have recently become increasingly knowledgeable about roofing products, with many of their staff attending courses provided by manufacturers to raise product awareness. The levels of stock and the depth of knowledge within branches varies widely, depending on how deeply they are involved in roofing materials, but, in general, their ranges should be greater than in the superstores.

Roofing Merchants

Some roofing contractors also operate as merchants and there are also specialist roofing merchants who cater for the trade. Not every town has one and so they are not always as accessible as the builders' merchants, but, if you are lucky enough to have one in your area, this is where you will find the most stock and knowledge. But, if you require something which is not in stock, generally the staff will know what you are talking about and be able to get it for you fairly quickly.

Manufacturers

Some manufacturers will sell direct to the public and some small firms, but many will not, preferring to sell to a network of merchants and to particular customers only. Few manufacturers and suppliers are now without a web site and a quick search on the product name should soon lead you to stockists or appropriate sales departments.

CHAPTER 3

Roof Types, Details and Design Considerations

This chapter deals with the different types of pitched roof, such as mono-pitch, duo-pitch, lean-to, gables, hips and valleys, and also raises the need to consider weight, pitch, planning and exposure when choosing materials and suitable fixing methods.

ROOF TYPES AND TERMINOLOGY

Single-Pitched Roofs

Mono-Pitched Roofs
The main aspect to consider with single-pitched roofs is how you are going to finish off at the top edges? For a mono-pitch roof, the most common method is to use special mono-pitch ridge tiles, which are easily obtained from tile manufacturers or roofing merchants.

Lean-To Roofs
For a lean-to roof the top edge is likely to be finished with a lead flashing.

Duo-Pitched Roofs
You will hear roofers describe a duo-pitched roof as a 'straight roof', a 'gable-to gable' or an 'up and over', among other terms. In the majority of these the rafters are designed to be equal in length on both sides, but they can differ, either by accident or design and so it is always wise to check before ordering materials or starting work.

Hips and Valleys

Hips
Hips are an alternative way of finishing the ends of a roof instead of gables. There is more work and more skill involved in finishing a hip than a verge, and they do cut down the storage or living space within, so these factors should be considered if you are having a house or an extension built.

Valleys
Valleys are the junctions that are formed when a part of a building, and therefore the roof, comes off another at right angles. Small valley sections are commonly known as 'pediments' or 'pikes'.

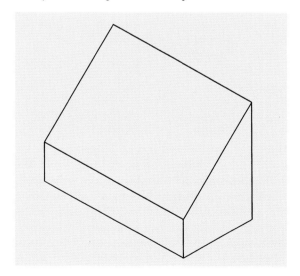

Mono-pitched roof.

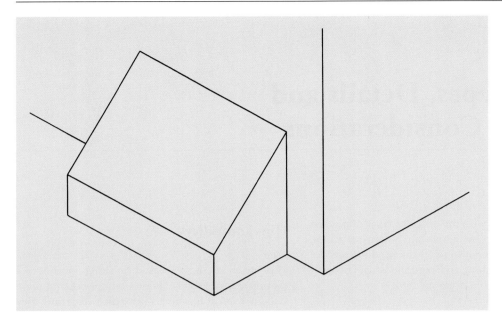

Lean-to roof.

DESIGN CONSIDERATIONS

This section deals with matters such as fixing specifications, roof pitch and the suitability of materials.

Weight

With a new roof the architect or designer has the responsibility to ensure that its structure is planned

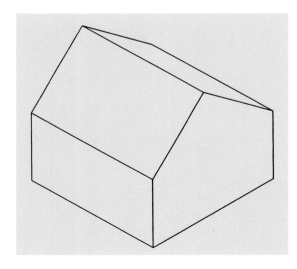

Straight verge-to-verge duo-pitched roof.

with the covering materials in mind; but, if you are re-roofing a property, then you need to check that the roof is strong enough to take the replacement materials. The first consideration here is the weight per square metre of the new tiles or slates compared with that of the existing covering. The suppliers of the new slates or tiles should all have technical departments to assist with such enquiries and are a good place to start if you do have concerns.

Pitch

All slates and tiles have a minimum recommended roof pitch, as stated by the supplier or manufacturer. If the products are laid below this pitch and the roof subsequently fails then any warranties will almost certainly be void. It is therefore essential to check the roof pitch and the minimum pitch of the slates or tiles. For some interlocking tiles this can be as low as 15 degrees, with plain tiles starting at 35 degrees.

The minimum pitch for any natural or artificial slate depends very much on the size of the slates and the location. The minimum pitch for any double-lap slating is actually only 20 degrees, but there are many design factors that go into this and so, in reality, this is rarely seen; a more realistic minimum pitch for most slates is around 27.5 degrees, but even this depends on certain conditions. Generally, slates, and

Roof with hips and valleys.

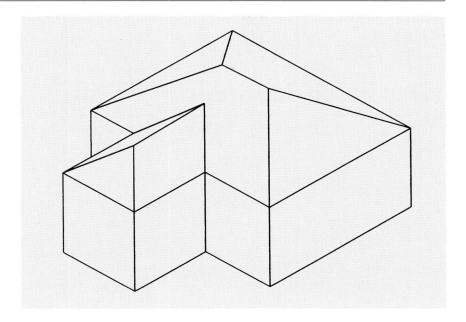

especially natural ones, are much 'happier' at steeper pitches of 35 to 40 degrees and upwards. Again, technical departments are a good source of information if you are not sure.

Fixing Specifications

It is worth remembering that pitch, location and the type of product (among other factors) can affect a fixing specification quite dramatically. You must make sure that the correct nails, clips or other fastenings are used in accordance with the specification recommended by the supplier, manufacturer or some other person responsible for the specification. Failure to adhere to a fixing specification can result in the loss of warranty, should the roof suffer any structural damage (such as the loss of slates or tiles).

Slates

Broadly speaking, the fixing specifications for natural slates are fairly straightforward (for instance, two nails or per slate), as they are for artificial slates (two nails plus a disc rivet), because each slate is fixed.

Plain Tiles

Traditionally, the fixing specification for plain tiles has also remained fairly standard across the country for many years. For roof pitches up to 60 degrees, the minimum recommended specification has been two nails in all perimeter tiles and each tile on every fifth course. Vertical surfaces and all roofs set above 60 degrees require two nails per tile wherever possible.

Interlocking Tiles

The fixing specifications for interlocking tiles have, over the years, ranged from, for instance, being simply perimetrically nailed, to every tile being nailed and clipped, depending on the type of tile used, the roof pitch and the location. This variation has been caused largely by the fact that there are so many different types (shapes, sizes and weights) available. A common method was needed and a group of leading British manufacturers have addressed this by agreeing and producing a zonal fixing guide for all their roof tiles. The required fixing specification may be found by using simple tables that rely on information such as the tile type, roof pitch and the location of the work. The guide is freely available from all of the major tile manufacturers and is relatively simple to use. However, to be on the safe side, I would still recommend that you should contact a technical department to make sure that you get the right fixing specification.

CHAPTER 4

First Essential Steps

This chapter describes the checks that should be made on the substructure (for instance, brickwork and joinery work) before starting and how to identify and solve potential problems. It also contains a checklist for planning the work through to the disposing of the waste and explains some setting-out principles common to all covering materials (that is, slates and tiles).

CHECKING THE ROOF

Checking the Roof for Square

All straight roofs (that is, verge-to-verge or verge to abutment) should be checked for square early in the process to avoid problems later on. Here are the checks that you should make and why you should make them.

Rafter Lengths
Rafter lengths should normally be of equal length at both ends of the roof, especially on roofs that have been formed by using modern factory-made trusses. Traditional 'cut' roofs rely much more heavily on the skill and accuracy of the person cutting and fixing the timbers, and so even the best examples may be slightly out. Old roofs in particular may be out by quite a way due to the movement and distortion that can occur over the years. In any case, it is always wise to check the rafter lengths for consistency. The price for not doing so may be the necessity to strip back some or all of the battens that you have so carefully fixed in place (and, as an unwelcome side effect, the underlay will be full of holes where the nails have been).

By using a tape measure, note the length of the left-hand rafter from the ridge down to the edge of the fascia board. Alternatively, it is acceptable to fix the first course batten and measure to the top edge of that instead of the fascia board. Repeat the process on the right-hand side and compare the measurements. If the difference is only slight (a few millimetres) you will not need to make any adjustments to the battening gauges and the top course of battens will finish parallel to the ridge, thus ensuring a correct finish when the roof is tiled. However, any significant difference in the measurements will result in the top batten slanting towards or away from the ridge rather than being parallel to it. Apart from the obvious visual problem, this can cause difficulties when it comes to fixing the tiles. Later, in the product-specific chapters, I shall describe exactly how to deal with this situation for each type of tile or slate, but, in general, the difference is split evenly throughout a number of gauges by reducing the gauge slightly on one end. This ensures that the battens can then be fixed in such a way that the gradual adjustment is not visible to the naked eye.

Ridge and Eaves' Lengths
This applies to straight roofs only. On a straight verge-to-verge roof it is unlikely that the ridge length will be exactly equal to the eaves' length and it is important to know how much difference there is before we begin to lay any roof tiles. As with the rafter lengths, a few millimetres here or there are not going to make much difference, but, if there is a significant difference, then adjustments to the joinery work may be necessary.

Out of square roofs (exaggerated for clarity).

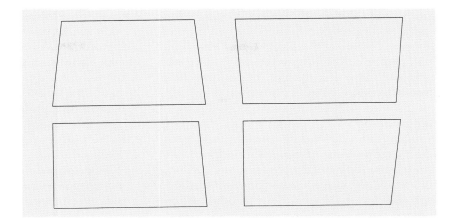

Out of square roofs – how to 'run' the undercloak.

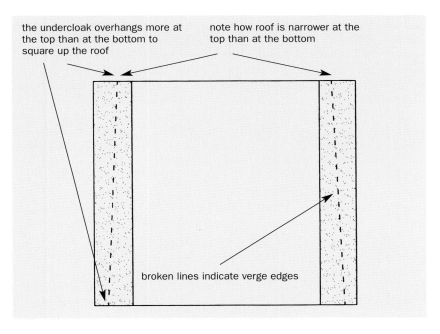

the undercloak overhangs more at the top than at the bottom to square up the roof

note how roof is narrower at the top than at the bottom

broken lines indicate verge edges

But, before you set about altering the joinery work, it may be possible to fix the problem during the 'setting/marking out' process by fixing the undercloak at a slight 'running' angle to square the roof back up. For example, if we overhang the undercloak 38mm over at the bottom and 50mm over at the top, we have squared the roof up by 24mm (12mm each side). While 'running' the undercloak in/out can come in handy, it should only be used to get you out of a problem; where possible it is better to keep the overhangs equal and open/close or in

some cases cut the slates or tiles (*see* product-specific sections).

Right Angles Check

You would probably think that, if the rafters are the same length and the eaves and ridge are equal, then the roof would be square. Not necessarily, the roof could be shaped like any of the examples in the illustrations above. It is important that the verges (bargeboards) are running at right angles to the eaves (fascia) so that the battens are fixed square and

31

parallel, ready for the slates or tiles. A verge which is not at 90 degrees (running off) can result in an unsightly twisting of the slates or tiles when laid, sometimes referred to as 'sore-toothing'. On pediments and valley sections it is the ridge line that needs to be square, rather than the eaves.

Builder's Square

If you have a builder's square or any flat, rectangular object that you know has right angles on it, the checking process will take only a few seconds. Simply place the square in the bottom corners of the roof, with one edge on the fascia board and the other in line with the bargeboard and perform a quick visual check for square.

The 3, 4, 5 Method

Another tried and tested way of checking for right angles is to use the 3, 4, 5 method, based on Pythagoras's theory. I shall avoid going into mathe-matics because this would just confuse the issue, suffice it to say that this method has long been known and is used in many operations across construction, and this is how we are going apply it.

1. Start at the outer corner of the fascia/barge junction and measure back 1200mm along the fascia and mark this point.
2. Then measure up the bargeboard 900mm and mark that point.
3. Now simply measure between the points and, if the junction is square, the diagonal measurement should be 1500mm.

This is just an example; you can use any measurements you like as long as they stay in the 3:4:5 ratio. Do not get too concerned if this is slightly out, the tiles or slates will still lay perfectly well provided the junctions are reasonably square. If your checks show that the roof is significantly out of square, you may

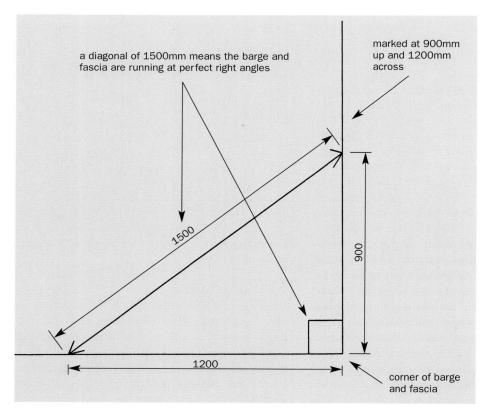

a diagonal of 1500mm means the barge and fascia are running at perfect right angles

marked at 900mm up and 1200mm across

1500

900

1200

corner of barge and fascia

How to check for square using the 3, 4, 5 method.

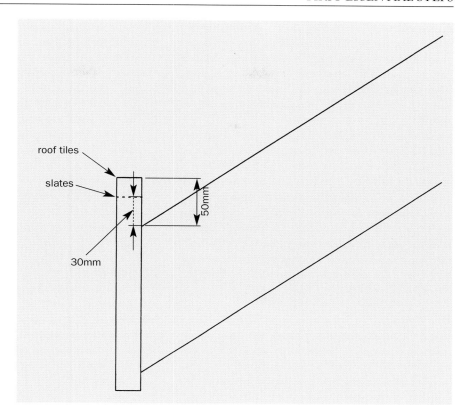

Fascia board heights for different materials.

roof tiles

slates

50mm

30mm

need to consider correcting this before carrying on. However, depending on the materials being used, there are a few tricks of the trade, which can be used so we shall look at how to deal with out-of-square roofs in the product-specific sections.

Fascia and Bargeboard Heights

Fascia Boards

The minimum upstand height at the fascia board (plus any over-fascia ventilation strips, if used) needs to be about 30mm for slates and 50mm for roof tiles. The angle of the slates or tiles on the bottom course should be at least the same as those on the main roof, or there should be a slight upwards tilt at the eaves, often referred to as a kick.

Perhaps the most reliable way to check fascia boards for height is actually to pin (that is, nailed but not fully driven) a couple of short pieces of batten into place and see how the bottom two courses look

when laid. If the bottom course drops away, you may need to increase the fascia height. Often the simplest way to do this is to fix a batten to the top edge of the fascia (often called a kick-lath or batten).

If the opposite problem exists and the roof kicks up sharply, the bottom course may end up too flat, which means that water will not run off properly and the area could leak. In this case the fascia may need to be replaced or dropped down to improve the run-off into the gutter. If adjustments are required they should be done place before you fix any permanent battens, because alterations afterwards will affect how much the tiles or slates overhang into the gutter.

Bargeboards

Bargeboards should finish flush (level) with the line of the rafters. This can be easily checked by eye, or by running a straight edge along to check the alignment. A flush finish means that the batten ends will be fully supported and allow any undercloak (if used) to sit at

33

the correct angle. If the bargeboard is below the line of the rafter it will fall away slightly, but this is not necessarily a problem and, in fact, it may actually help to drain water that runs down the verge away from the building. Having the bargeboards too high has the opposite effect and therefore should be avoided.

Although technically incorrect in most circumstances, in some areas it is fairly common practice to set the bargeboards up by 25mm above the end rafter so that the top edge is in line with the battens once they are fixed. This means that the undercloak (if applicable) goes on top of the battens rather than under them. If you encounter this, you will have to take one of the tile nibs off to get the tile to sit properly (right-hand side one for right verge, left-hand for left verge). The alternative, of course, is to have the joinery work corrected.

Brickwork

In most standard forms of construction there will be brickwork or some other masonry at the gable ends and party walls between the properties, if they are terraced or semi-detached. It is important to ensure that none of the brickwork is above the rafter line since this can damage the underlay or interfere with the battens. As with the bargeboards, this can be checked by eye or by running a straight edge down the rafters and over the brickwork.

Planning the Job

Most slating and tiling jobs should follow the same pattern of scaffold erection (by a competent person only), felting (underlay) and battening, setting or marking out, the fixing of any background components (such as undercloak or valley liners), loading out followed by the fixing of the slates or tiles and finally any mortar work or dry fix details. The final part of the process is the tidying up and the safe disposal of any waste.

This may all seem quite straightforward, but it is well worth going through the job in your mind first to ensure that:

- the working platform (scaffold) is erected on time and is fully complete and to your needs;

- a suitable skip is on hire or, if you are tipping the waste, that you have contacted the local authorities to do this in line with the regulations;
- any plant you may require is available and suitable for your needs (such as disc cutters or mixers);
- you avoid foot traffic on the slates or tiles once laid; there are too many possibilities to go into, but typically you should try to avoid tiling or slating the whole roof in and coming back to it, instead, try to complete details such as hips, valleys or ridge as the slates or tiles are brought through as this normally allows you to work off the battens; there will times when this might not be practicable or possible and in this case you should use a roofer ladder.

Materials Check

This again is a fairly obvious thing to do, but I have seen many jobs delayed and working hours lost because the materials were not checked first. It is a simple matter of checking the materials delivered against the list that you need to do the work. I recommend something along the lines of:

- roof tiles (or slates): check quantity and colour or finish and breakages (if possible);
- fittings (ridge tiles, verge tiles, for instance): as above;
- battens: check size and quantities;
- underlay (felt): check number of rolls and for any damage;
- mortar materials (if used): check that cement has no hard lumps, availability of a clean water supply and plasticizer and check ratio of sand (ideally sharp sand) to cement (3:1);
- dry fix and ventilation components: check that there are instructions, fixing kits (screws, clips, for instance) and enough of each component, including any stop ends and end capping pieces, for example;
- fixings: check that the nails and clips, for example, are correct for the materials you are using and are sufficient in quantity;
- lead (if used): check that the code is correct and for size and quantities (see chapter 10 on basic flashings).

CHAPTER 5

Installing Background Materials

This chapter describes how common materials used on slated and tiled roofs should be fixed. Any slight variations between the different materials will be dealt with in their specific chapters.

UNDERLAY (FELT)

Eaves

As indicated previously, most slating and tiling underlays are not designed to be exposed to the elements and so it is important that felt-support trays (sidelap normally 150mm) are used to conduct water into the gutter, with the underlay set back out of harm's way. Another popular method of treating the eaves is to use a membrane that has been designed for exposure, such as Type 5U (a flat roofing felt). When using 5U, it is normally deemed sufficient to cut the roll in half (width-wise) and use a 500mm strip along the eaves rather than the full 1m roll. The leading edge of the 5U should extend approximately halfway into the gutter. Again, the leading edge of the underlay can then be set back. Where possible, the first strip of underlay across the roof should be all in one piece (that is, not jointed). The eaves are an area where water can gather if there are defects in the roof (such as broken or missing tiles), so avoid nailing in the bottom 200mm or so.

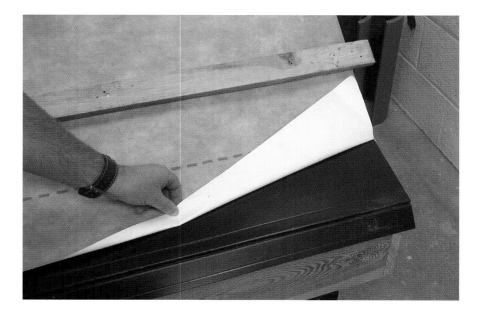

Felt-support trays at eaves with underlay set back.

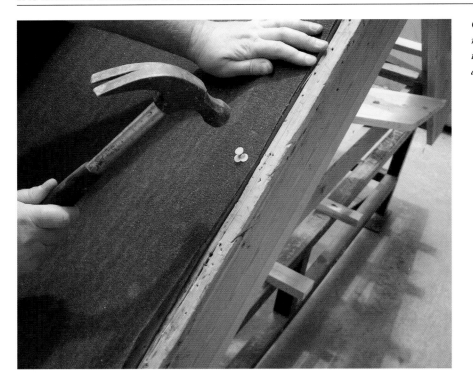

Cluster of nails near centre of the roll to create a pivot.

Underlay rolled out, straightened and fixed.

To help in getting the underlay straight and level when rolling out, fix a small cluster of nails or staples about halfway down the edge of the roll to act as a pivot, rather than use a line of fixings. Roll the underlay out across several rafters before straightening it and adding additional fixings.

Joints

When one roll stops part-way across the roof there are several ways of forming a joint to carry on the process. The important point is that no underlay should be left hanging about unsupported and that there is sufficient lap at the sides. To form a water-tight joint, start by trimming off or folding back the surplus underlay and then start the next roll one full rafter back.

Horizontal Laps

The horizontal lap from one strip of underlay to the next depends on the pitch of the roof and on whether or not the roof is boarded, but the standard minimal headlap is normally 150mm. Most modern underlays actually come with the lap line already marked on, but, if this is not the case, it is a good idea to strike horizontal lines to maintain a consistent lap and to help in keeping the underlay straight.

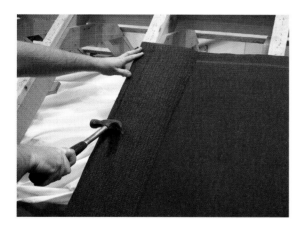

ABOVE: Fold or cut off the underlay back where it overhangs a rafter.

ABOVE RIGHT: Start the next roll, one full rafter back to form a watertight joint.

RIGHT: Horizontal laps are normally 150mm for most roof pitches.

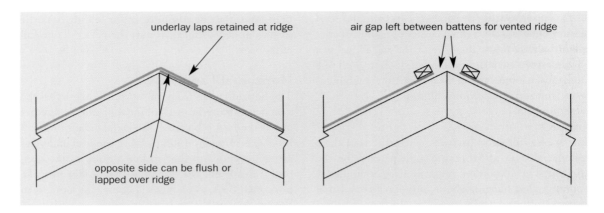

Underlay to ridge, lapped over and set down for ventilated ridge.

At the Ridge

Much depends on the specification and the type of underlay used in determining how it finishes at the ridge. Most ventilated ridge details require the underlay to be set down at about 30 to 50mm on each side from the ridge to leave a clear air gap, while in standard, non-ventilated ridge details the common practice is to position one side level with the ridge and carry the other over the top by the same minimal lap (for example, 150mm) as has been used for the rest of the roof.

Underlay lay at hips, lapped at 150mm parallel to hip rafter.

At the Hips

The hips can be finished in much the same way as the ridge, with a minimal 150mm lap, but this time being measured over the hip rafter rather than the ridge line. Alternatively, both sides of the underlay may be trimmed on to the hip rafter, fixed in place and then covered by a continuous strip (minimum 600mm wide).

At the Valley

For GRP valley liners the most common method is to fix a continuous, 1m strip of underlay down the valley, to give an even 500mm on each side. To roll underlay down a valley can be difficult, as well as slightly hazardous, and so to make the task safer and simpler measure the length you need (measure the middle of the valley and add about 3m) and cut it on the floor or scaffold. Then fold and crease it down the centre; this makes positioning and fixing much easier, especially when you are working in twos.

Technically speaking, all underlay should be cut back from exposure, but doing this at the base of the valley may leave it vulnerable to leaks. Thus in this case it is better to allow the continuous strip of underlay to come right down to extend over the fascia board and be trimmed halfway into the gutter.

The adjacent underlay is then cut or folded to the sides of the valley liner (once positioned) or, if specified, lapped on to it.

Underlay trimmed to side of GRP valley.

If the valley is lead-lined there should be no underlay at all beneath the lead. This is because the underlay could actually melt when the lead gets hot, thus trapping any water that gets in. The underlay should be lapped on to the sides of the lead as shown.

Underlay to valley.

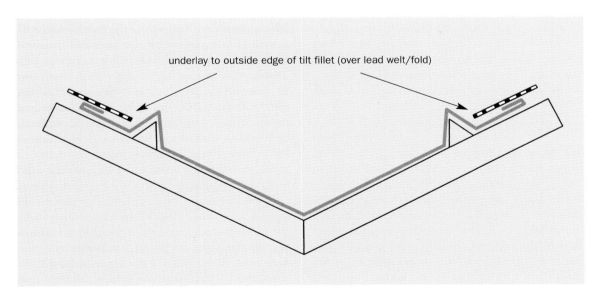

underlay to outside edge of tilt fillet (over lead welt/fold)

Underlay lapped on to (rather than under) lead valleys.

Upstands against abutments (100mm).

Upstands

At walls or chimneys, for instance, it is good practice to turn the underlay up because it adds to the water tightness of that particular detail. In general, you should aim to turn the underlay up by at least 100mm; but, depending on the roof covering, this may prove too much but it is better too high than too low because it is much easier to trim than to reinstall.

BATTENS

Marking up Gauges (in Sets)

One of the biggest mistakes that people make when marking up gauges is to do them one at a time. I have seen many trainees and inexperienced roofers scratching their heads and wondering why the top batten is running out by 30 or 40mm when they have checked the roof and all the battens and then just cannot find the error. What has normally happened is that they have marked one batten at a time and have made a number of tiny errors of 2 or 3mm each time they have transferred the tape. Marking gauges

in sets saves time and is more accurate. For example, the maximum gauge for plain tiles on a pitched roof is normally 100mm. This means that there are ten courses per metre. If the roof is 5m long there will be around fifty courses. Marking one at a time means that there are fifty chances to get it slightly wrong. Theoretically, if one side of the roof is marked at 101mm and the other side at 99mm, then the roof could run out by 100mm, which is equal to one full course of tiles. Normally it is possible to fit about eight plain or nine tile courses on each strip of underlay, so this means that the same roof could be marked in six sets (multiples of 100mm). Suddenly there are fewer chances to make mistakes. Now, even if every set is out by 2mm (one high, one low) the battens will run out by only 10 to 12mm.

In reality, plain tiles are not normally a problem because the gauge is so simple, but I have used them as an example because the high number of courses makes it easier to illustrate the point about the risk of mistakes. The problem comes mainly in tiles and slates with gauges that can be adjusted, or if the gauge

Batten joints and nails should aim for the centre of the rafter.

is an awkward one (for instance, 328mm rather than a neat 330mm). The fact is that all slate and tile gauges should be marked up in sets irrespective of the gauge; we shall cover this further in the product-specific sections.

Cutting and Fixing

General

Apart from the narrowest parts of a hip or valley, batten sections should be at least 1200mm long and span two rafters (three fixing points). When jointing battens, they should be neatly sawn and fixed on to the centre of the rafter with the nails angled slightly inwards. Always try and nail close to the central point where the batten crosses over the rafter, this avoids unwanted splits and missed fixings.

Joints

When working on trussed roofs, it is important that the joints be regularly staggered (that is, not all in a line) to brace the roof for added strength and to avoid splitting the truss. The rule is that no more than one in four joints should be on the same rafter for gauges

over 200mm (for instance, interlocking tiles) and no more than three in twelve for gauges under that (for instance, medium or small slates and plain tiles).

If you are working on a traditional 'cut' roof the rafters are normally a good deal wider than the trusses and the whole structure is independently stronger, so there is no real necessity to stagger the joints. However, to be on the safe side I would still advise some staggering of the joints. The simplest way to do this is to move the line of the joints to another rafter for each new strip of underlay.

At Hips and Valleys

At the hips, the batten ends should be cut to an angle, be fully supported by the hip rafter or timber

Battens should be fully supported and nailed at hips.

noggins and securely nailed. The treatment at valleys depends much on the formation, but the same rules apply in that the ends should be angled, supported and securely fixed. Ideally, all valley construction details should include noggins. These are supporting timbers set back parallel to the centre of the valley and which provide excellent fixing points for the batten ends. Unfortunately, this is one 'luxury' that does not arise nearly often enough now, so the only alternative for most roofers is either to install the noggins themselves or to 'skew' nail into the sides of the battens or valley boards.

Fixing to Masonry

Occasionally, you may need to fix to walls, especially if you are doing some vertical plain tiling to gable ends. Normally, the best way to do this is not to try and batten straight to the wall, but to drill, plug and screw counter battens to the wall first. The maximum centres (that is, the spacing between corresponding edges) should be no more than 450mm. The battens can then be fixed as normal.

COUNTER BATTENS

These are timbers (normally 50mm × 50mm) fixed in line with the rafters before the normal battens are installed. The main purpose of counter battens is to increase the flow of air in the roof and thereby reduce the risk of condensation. Counter battens tend to be specified mostly on roofs that are insulated at rafter level (over rafter insulation boards or between rafter insulation set down to rafter level). Whether the counter battens go on before or on top of the underlay depends largely on where the airflow needs to be directed, so you should always check the specification.

PREFORMED VALLEY LINERS

General

Individual manufacturers have their own fixing instructions, which you must follow to ensure that you are fitting the products in line with the warranties. The general procedure though is very similar. Ideally, the valley section should be boarded out by

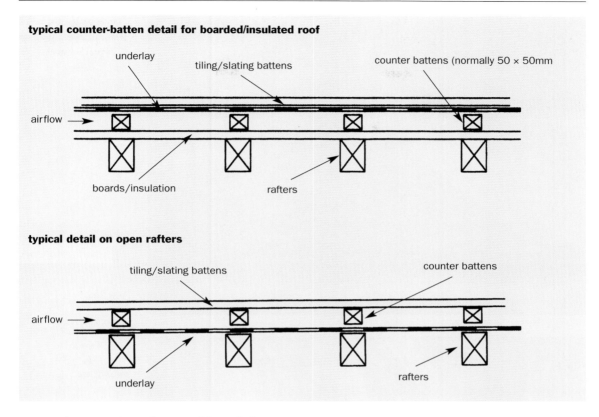

typical counter-batten detail for boarded/insulated roof

underlay

tiling/slating battens

counter battens (normally 50 × 50mm

airflow

boards/insulation

rafters

typical detail on open rafters

tiling/slating battens

counter battens

airflow

underlay

rafters

Counter battens under and on top of the underlay.

the joiner so that the boards (19 to 25mm deep) are dropped in between and at the same level of the rafters. Alternatively, the valley can be boarded out on top of the rafters by using 6mm plywood (or similar). The second method is less labour-intensive, cheaper and can be done by roofers and so tends to be the more common of the two. These valleys tend to be about 400mm wide (200mm each side), so, to ensure support for both the valley liner and the batten ends, the plywood boards should be at least 225mm wide on each side.

Most GRP valleys benefit from having the fascia boards (or over fascia vent strips) notched out to allow them to retain their shape as they come through to the gutter. Notching should be done before the guttering is fixed to ensure that it is not set too high. If you are unable to take a notch out of the

fascia then the valley will flatten, be under stress and the tiles or slates will kick at the eaves. The only alternative to notching is to draw the edge of the valley back from where it begins to break and install a lead saddle from code 4 lead or better. Where two valleys meet at the top (that is, at the ridge) then they should be cut as tightly together as possible and finished with a lead saddle.

Bedded and Non-Bedded Valleys

GRP valley liners are normally installed on battens fixed to the outer edges and which run parallel to the centre of the valley. The battens on the main roof should then be cut (at an angle) to the sides of the valley battens and secured to either a noggin, nearby rafter or one of the valley battens.

Notching the fascia allows GRP valleys to retain their shape.

GRP valley liner supported on battens.

Dry Valleys

In recent years several dry valley systems have come on to the market. Dry valleys have a raised section running full length down the middle of the liner. The slates and tiles will be cut to this and fixing kits, including clips and instructions, are normally supplied as standard. These valleys tend to be fixed direct to the boarding (in-set boards or plywood) with the battens from the main roof overlapping the edges of the liner.

HIP IRONS

The leading edge of the hip iron should be set approximately 50mm over the fascia board so that it comes in line with the bottom edges of the tiles or slates. The leading corners of the first hip tile will then be cut to this same angle to ensure a correct finish. One common mistake is to set the hip iron back to avoid having to cut the end hip tile. This is poor practice and can result in a leak where the fascia boards join below the hip iron.

UNDERCLOAK

Bargeboards and, in some cases, gable end brickwork are prone to deviation in their length, just like the fascia boards at the eaves, and this can transfer itself to the verge detail when installing the undercloak. For this reason it is advisable to lay undercloak to a line, especially on longer rafters. If you are using fibre-cement strips of uniform width, measure the required overhang and mark the width of the undercloak on the top and the bottom batten (for instance, 50mm over 150mm). Strike a line between the points and fix the inside edge of the undercloak to this.

If you are using verge clips, then you fix the top and bottom ones, suspend a line between them and use the line as a guide for the outer edge of the undercloak. This is especially useful when using undercloak of non-uniform width or when the undercloak needs bedding.

If you are not using verge clips, attach short lengths of batten fixed to the top and bottom of the verge and saw notches (or tack in nails) at the required overhang. Use the notches or nails to suspend the line between the two points.

ABOVE: *Hip irons should extend into the gutter.*

BELOW: *Uniform width undercloak laid to strike line.*

Undercloak fixed to a line suspended between verge clips.

Bedded Undercloaks

Before bedding an undercloak it is important to make sure that the brickwork or stonework at the gable end is correct. It should be cut neatly to a line about 10mm below the rafter line for a slate or fibre-cement strip undercloak, or about 25mm for plain tile undercloak. If the masonry has not been cut neatly to a line and comes level with or above the rafter line in places, this will result in a wavy and sometimes cracked undercloak and, in turn, noticeable deviations in the verge slates or tiles.

To install the undercloak, first determine the overhang (*see* the sections on setting out). If the roof has already been battened, ease up the batten ends care-

fully so that the undercloak may be inserted beneath them. If verge clips are to be used, then they should be fixed to the batten ends with the outer edges to the line, before they are eased up. Bed the wall so that it is about 25mm higher than the rafter line. Slide the undercloak into place so that the outer edge is level with the line and tap down with a straight edge until the desired level is reached. Normally, a bedded undercloak goes under the underlay, but in some cases may this be specified the other way around. The important thing in either case is to provide a good key for the mortar, so, if the underlay intrudes into the mortar, then trim it back. Finally, tap down the batten ends.

Nailed Undercloaks

Plain tiles are not normally suitable for nailing as undercloaks and so the following applies to slates and fibre-cement strips only. For an undercloak to be nailed there has to be something to nail it to, and this is normally an end rafter finished with a bargeboard. The bargeboard should be level with or even a fraction lower than the end rafter so that the undercloak is properly supported and does not tilt inwards towards the roof when laid. Slates should be nailed at least twice per piece, and fibre-cement strips should be nailed at each end, plus two or more other places towards the centre. There needs just to be sufficient fixings to hold it in place until the batten ends are nailed through. Undercloak should be fixed into the end rafter (rather than the bargeboard) with large-headed clout nails.

Cutting and Positioning Pieces (Fibre-Cement Strips only)

At the eaves there is normally a tilting fillet, which fills the gap between the bargeboard and the top of the fascia. The machined edge of the undercloak should start from here, and the top should be cut off at the apex by nibbling with slate cutters or by scribing and snapping. The piece at the eaves should then be installed by putting a machined edge to the junction and cutting the leading edge halfway on to the fascia board. Drawing the edge back from the edge of the fascia by a few millimetres means that the line of the fascia board is not affected by the thickness of the undercloak (approximately 6mm) and so the slate or

Undercloak to eaves.

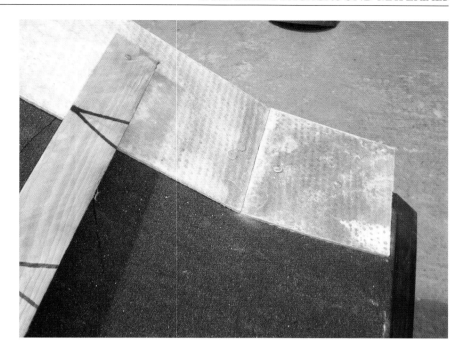

tile can come through at the verge without lifting. Ideally, the undercloak should extend over the fascia board to meet the edge of the slate or tile, but this requires that the fascia board is notched out to the width of the undercloak and to a depth of around 25mm, which is not always practicable, especially if the guttering has already been fixed into place. Small sections are quite fragile and may crack if you try to nail straight through, so it is better to form the holes first.

MORTAR (MIXING AND USING)

Use and Consistency

Mortar for roofing work should be used within two hours of mixing; adding water to 'knock-up' the mix should be avoided because this can affect the strength. Its consistency should be much firmer than that of bricklaying mortar (almost like very soft clay), with the possible exception of the mortar for pointing, which is normally mixed slightly softer for ease of use.

It is important to get the consistency of bedding mortar correct; it needs to be firm enough to 'stand up' rather than slump once positioned, but it should not be so dry that it is unworkable. A good firm mortar helps with compaction when tiles are pressed on to it, which, in turn, helps the mortar bed to withstand the vibration caused by nailing or clipping. The fact that the bed is quite solid also makes pointing-up much easier.

Bedding and pointing should be carried out as soon as possible and certainly in the same working day to ensure that the two parts bond together properly.

When bedding and pointing ridge or hip tiles in hot conditions it is advisable to soak the tiles in clean water for a couple of minutes first. This is especially important when using clay materials, which can draw the water out of the mortar mix quite rapidly. If the mortar dries out too quickly then it will shrink, crack and not achieve full strength. It is important to ensure that the mix is used within two hours or thrown away. Do not add extra water to a mix later on as this will reduce the strength.

CLIPS

General

Clips are specified when nailing alone is not deemed sufficient to keep the slates and tiles securely on the roof. Some product ranges have to be clipped in all specifications, but normally additional clipping is required when the roof reaches a certain pitch or is located in an area with particularly high wind speeds. In some cases, the better-safe-than-sorry philosophy comes into play, so many clients opt for additional clipping even when the minimal fixing specification does not call for it.

ABOVE: *Typical tile clip, fixed over interlock and into the batten.*

BELOW: *Typical eaves clip, fixed over interlock and into the fascia.*

Verge Clips

Verges form one of the most vulnerable parts of the roof, and tiles and slates can easily be lost from these areas in high winds. The purpose of a verge clip is, of course, to prevent this and, if installed correctly, it is a job they perform very well. All verge clips have two nail holes and should therefore be nailed twice with the inside edge of the clip lined up with the outer edge undercloak. Fix one verge clip per course per side, with the exception of the top course, which does not need one. Some manufacturers provide the nails (often ribbed) in a fixing kit, depending on the type of slate or tile on the roof; but, where this is not the case, the nails should be 20mm galvanized, large-headed clout or similar.

Tile Clips

These are used to prevent the tails from lifting in high winds and other extreme pressure conditions such as vortices from large aircraft. Most tile clips work by hooking around the interlock and then being nailed into a batten. This ensures that the tail of the tile that is clipped benefits from a much greater resistance to wind uplift.

Some tile clips also tie two tiles together, while others are a clip and a nail in one. There are, in fact, a number of variations and so it is important to check with the manufacturer or supplier that you have the right clips and know how to fix them.

Eaves Clips

This is simply a clip specifically made for the eaves to perform the same job as a tile clip. Again, there are many variations so check that you have the right ones for the tiles.

CHAPTER 6

Interlocking Tiles

By covering such matters as many of the common materials and general setting out in earlier chapters, we may now concentrate on specific material types. Each of the following four chapters (on interlocking tiles, plain tiles, natural slates and artificial slates) will include working out gauges, the positioning of battens and how to install these materials to the various common details.

There is a body of knowledge and many transferable skills between the several types of slate and tile, and so, to avoid repetition, I have made this first specific section the most extensive, not least because interlocking tiles form the largest part of the market and are the most commonly used on new-build sites, extensions and re-roofing projects.

It is worth noting that the standard recommended (minimal) batten size for interlocking tiles is 50mm × 25mm, where the rafter centres exceed 450mm apart. Truss roofs are normally set at 600mm centres. Below 450mm rafter centres (which applies to most traditional 'cut' roofs) 38mm × 25mm battens may be used.

SETTING OUT

Battens, Fixed Points and Gauges

Finding the First Fixed Point
1. Turn the roof tile over and measure from the underside of the nib to the tail (in this case 395mm).
2. Take your tape or rule and extend the end of it 50mm over the fascia board (or halfway into the gutter, whichever is less).

3. Mark this at both ends of the roof and strike a line between the two points; note that the marks are made with 'arrows' and the line struck through the point for accuracy.
4. Fix the batten with the top edge to the line (just a few nails for now, not driven).

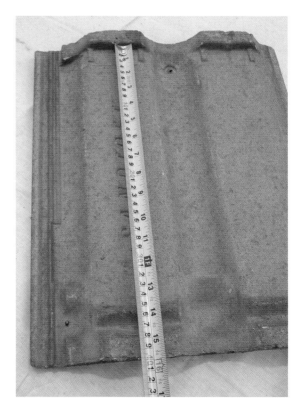

Tile measured from underside of nib to tail.

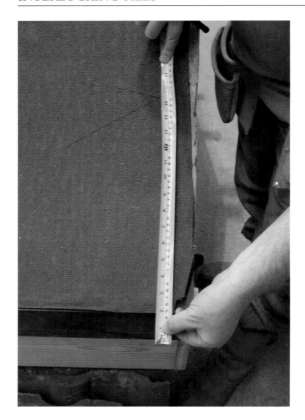

Setting the overhang over the fascia.

5. The top edge of this batten is the first fixed point; try a tile on at each end to make sure that it is overhanging correctly into the gutter before continuing.
6. You now have your first fixed point.

Finding the Second Fixed Point

1. Measure the thickness of the tile nib (in this case 25mm) or, if the nib is set down from the top, measure from the underside of the nib to the top of the tile.
2. Allow 5 to 10mm for clearance and make a mark (normally about 30 to 40mm) down from the apex or top of the rafter.
3. This mark will be the top edge of the top batten; you now have your second fixed point.

Note: it is always preferable to have the top fixed point as high as is practicably possible, but provided that the ridge tile or flashing covers the top edge of the tile by 75mm the top batten may be able to come down slightly if necessary.

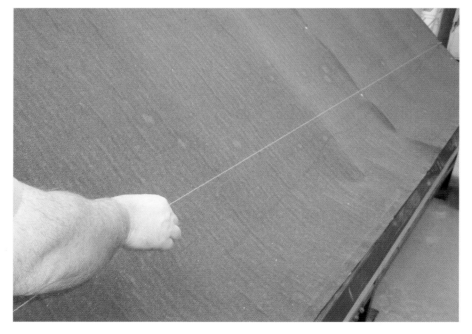

Marking and striking for the first course.

The top edge of the batten should touch the underside of the line.

BELOW: *Checking the overhang at each end with tiles.*

Nib thickness (or distance from the underside to the top of the tile).

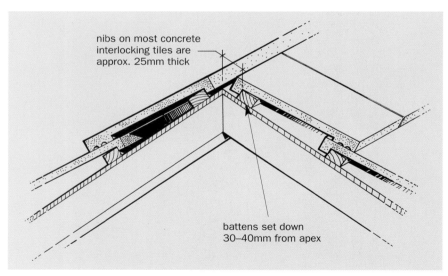

nibs on most concrete interlocking tiles are approx. 25mm thick

battens set down 30–40mm from apex

Mark down from the apex to allow clearance.

The Maximum Gauge

The term gauge or batten gauge refers to the distance between the courses when measured between corresponding points, that is, from the top edge of one batten to the top edge of the one above. This distance is also equal to the 'margin', the visible length of a tile (or slate) once laid. This is useful to know because, if you ever need to find out what gauge existing tiles or slates have been fixed at, you can just measure the margin. The maximum gauge of a roof tile may be found in the manufacturer's technical literature or from his web site. But, if you have access to neither

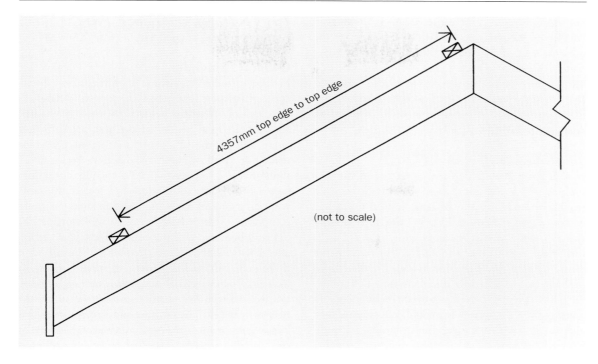

4357mm top edge to top edge

(not to scale)

Working out the even gauge.

but know the minimum headlap (normally 75mm), the maximum gauge may be found by using the formula:

length – lap = maximum gauge
(example: 420mm – 75mm = 345mm)

Working out the Even Gauge

1. It is important to know what the maximum is so that we do not exceed it; but what we are really interested in for variable gauge products, is to work out the even gauge so that the courses are spaced out consistently.
2. With a tape, measure between the two fixed points and record the distance in millimetres.
3. With a calculator, divide this distance by the maximum gauge to find out the number of courses, rounding up the answer to the next whole number (always round up unless the first figure after the decimal place is a zero, if this happens you may try up the maximum gauge to see if

it finishes high enough to be covered by the ridge tile or flashing; minimum 75mm); *example:* distance between fixed points = 4357mm; 4357mm ÷ 345mm = 12.63 (13 courses).
4. Now divide the distance again, but this time by the number of courses and round off to the nearest millimetre (up for ≥0.5 and down for ≤0.4); *example:* 4357mm ÷ 13 = 335.15mm (335mm).
5. This is the even gauge that you will use to batten up the roof.

Note: do not forget that in some roofs, especially old ones, the rafter lengths may vary slightly, so the gauges need to be checked at both ends and, if you have a duo-pitch, at both sides too; if the rafter is shorter, simply knock a few millimetres off each course and, if it is longer, add a few millimetres (but do not exceed the maximum gauge). You should aim to make the changes as even as possible by spreading the difference across all or most of the gauges, with the maximum addition or drop being around 5mm.

For example: using our earlier example of thirteen courses at 335mm, we find that the rafter at the opposite end of the roof is 50mm longer. You can either add 4mm to each course, which will increase the gauge to 339mm to make up 52mm (which is fine), or add 5mm to the last ten courses. If the rafter is shorter then the measurements are, of course, deducted rather than added.

Tricky Little Measurements?

If your gauge works out at a good round number such as 335 or 340mm, then you should have no trouble in marking the battens, but if the gauge works out at something like 337mm then finding this accurately on a tape can be quite tricky. This is one of the reasons many roofers still prefer imperial measurements. There is a simple way of resolving this problem and it takes only about a minute or so to do. First, cut a piece of batten just over a metre in length. Starting from the factory-sawn end, extend your tape and mark the first gauge (for instance, 337mm). Keeping the tape extended, add the next gauge (2 × 337mm = 674mm) and then a third (3 × 337mm = 1011mm). This gauge batten may now be used instead of a tape and will save you time and reduce the number of errors.

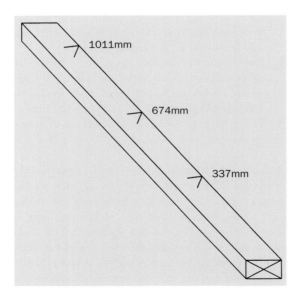

Making a gauge 'stick'.

SETTING OR MARKING OUT (ACROSS THE ROOF)

General Principle

In roofing there are, to put it mildly, many differences of opinion. These include regional differences and, indeed, differences from one roofing gang to another, no more so in setting and marking out. Some will claim that there is no need to set or mark out at all, others may disagree. Personally, I think that it is an essential part of the job, but it does take a little patience to learn and feel comfortable with. It is one of those things that looks far more complicated than it really is, but is well worth sticking with because, once the penny drops, your setting out skills will reduce the frequency of errors and make your work easier, faster and more pleasing to look at. When we talk about 'setting out' or 'marking out' we are referring to lines on the roof to lay the tiles or slates to. These lines are sometimes called 'perp' lines (short for perpendicular). A series of corresponding marks (typically three tiles wide) is made along the bottom and the top edge batten and a coloured line (chalk line or wet redline) is struck between the marks. These marks can then be used to load out the roof accurately, lay the tiles or slates in straight lines and to denote start or finishing positions, such as at the verges and either side of a valley.

Shunt (Opening and Closing Tiles)

All roof tiles that interlock can be shunted 'open' (laid wider) or 'closed' (laid tighter) and this is designed into the tiles for three main reasons. The first is so that the tiles can be opened or closed if the roof is out of square. The second reason is to adjust the width of the tiling to provide a suitable overhang at the verges (if using 'wet'/mortar finish), and the final reason is again to adjust the overall width of the tiling to try and work the roof into a full tile (that is, avoiding having to cut tiles at the verge). However, in my experience, if a cut tile looks likely you often need a long roof and/or some very generous shunt to avoid one, but it can prove a time-saver and so is sometimes worth a try.

ABOVE: Tiles shunted open.

BELOW: Tiles shunted to closed position.

Overhangs

The undercloak at the verges should extend between 38 and 50mm to comply with good practice guidance and the manufacturer's own technical information. However, in the real world it is quite acceptable to go a few more millimetres either way in the interests of common sense. You should, however, try to get as close to these measurements as possible, which may include shunting the tiles and using cut tiles, if need be. How conveniently the tiles come in at the verges is largely a matter of luck, since roofs are rarely designed to fit the roof tiles. Ideally, what you are looking for is a 'full tile' finish. This means that the tiles will lie within the limits of the shunt and the overhang at each end will be between 38 and 50mm. If you cannot achieve a full tile finish then introduce a cut of no less than half a tile wide at the right-hand side of the verge. Always try to use a cut that maintains the profile of the tiling. A cut tile alters the total width of the tiling, giving you another chance to achieve the required overhang.

The worst case scenario is that the cut tile still does not provide the correct overhangs, and so this means that the tiles at the left-hand verge will have to be cut as well. Again, always try to use a cut that maintains the profile of the tiling.

Thankfully, having to cut at both ends does not happen too often, and mainly on very small roofs where there are not enough tiles for the shunt to

BELOW: Typical right-hand 'starter' cut (discarded piece on right-hand side).

come into play or on jobs where there is no room for negotiation with the overhang limits.

Having explained what setting and marking out is, what shunt is and about the required overhangs, it is time to explain how the various roof types are marked out for interlocking tiles.

BASIC SETTING OUT FOR SMALL, STRAIGHT ROOFS

If you are just doing a small to medium-sized straight roof, such as a porch, garage or a main roof less than 5m wide, then the easiest way to set out is simply to run the tiles along the eaves and shunt them about until they fit and you are happy with the overhangs.

Of course, you might need to try a cut if this does not work to a full tile. You may be able to tile in the smaller jobs without striking lines, but for larger ones it may be wise to strike 'perp' lines.

To mark out by using this method start at the right-hand side (bottom course) and set the first tile (or cut) to the required overhang. Then tile along the eaves and shunt the tiles about until the overhang is correct at the other side of the roof. Leave the tiles in place and repeat the exercise on the top course.

Next, take out every third tile and mark the left-hand edges of the tiles (bottom and top courses) and, once you have done this right across the roof, take all the tiles off. Then strike lines between the corresponding marks to leave a set of 'perps' to lay your tiles to.

Typical left-hand 'finisher' cut (discarded piece on left-hand side).

Laying tiles out to establish the overhang at the verge.

Simple method of setting out with tiles (every third removed).

SETTING OUT FOR LARGER AND MORE COMPLICATED ROOFS

For this type of job the simple method described can be very time-consuming and so it is more common

for professional roofers to mark out by using a staff, or 'marking lath' as it is sometimes known. The idea is to mark three tile-widths on a batten and use this for setting out, rather than laying out tiles. Marking out in this way can take some grasping, but, if you can manage it, you will find that the ten or fifteen

58

minutes spent setting out is well worth it with regard to the speed and quality of the work.

Making a Marking Lath (Staff)

Follow this method to create a marking lath for any interlocking roof tile.

1. Lay a tile squarely on any batten and mark the left-hand edge; we will call this the 'first mark'.

2. Making sure that the first tile does not move, lay three tiles to the left of it, opening (but never forcing) each one to its full laying width, again, mark the left-hand edge.

3. Take off the three tiles and repeat the process, this time closing the tiles; mark the left-hand edge again and remove all the tiles.

4. You should now have two marks about 10mm apart; split the difference and make a mark

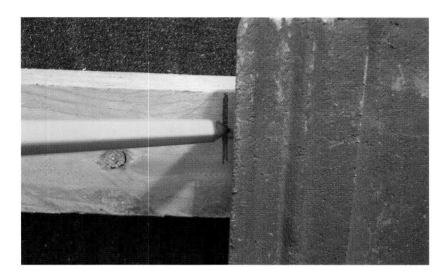

Marking the first tile.

Open and closed marks for three tiles.

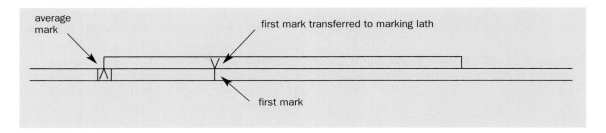

Picking up the first mark.

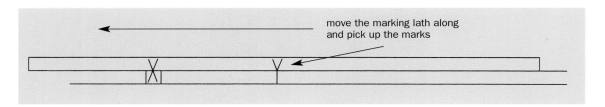

Picking up the next and other marks.

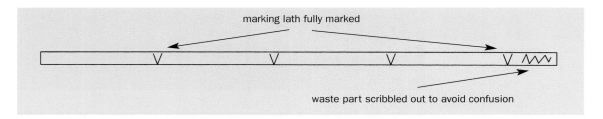

Completed marking lath.

in the middle, this will be the average tiling gauge.

5. Find a straight and fairly smooth batten (full length) to mark on and place one end level with the average mark, move along to the first mark you made and transfer this up to the marking batten.

6. Move the marking batten to the left until the mark you have just made comes into line with the average mark, again transfer the first mark you made up to the marking batten.

7. Continue until the batten is full and, with a pencil, scribble out the part which is spare to avoid confusion later on.

Marking out for Straight Roofs

Before we can put any marks on the roof we have to test it to establish factors such as overhang, whether we shall need cuts and anything out of square. Follow this method to find out what you need to know about the roof you are about to tile.

1. Place the marking batten on the bottom course batten with the end of it flush (level) with the outer edge of the left-hand bargeboard.

2. Move to the other end of the marking batten and transfer the furthest mark (since this is only a temporary mark, use a line not an arrow) on to the bottom course batten.

Start trying the roof through from flush with the left-hand verge.

Move the marks along until close to the right-hand verge.

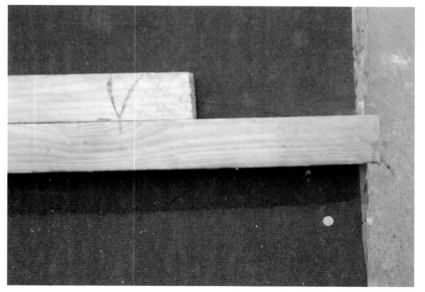

3. Keep moving the marking batten along in the same way until you get close to the right-hand verge.

4. At this point lay a tile (or a cut if required) on to the last mark and carry on laying tiles to the right of it until one carries over the right-hand verge; measure the total overhang and divide by two (averaging out the overhang).

5. If this is within or at least close to the overhang limits (38 to 50mm each side) go back to the left-hand side and place the end of the marking batten over at the required overhang; you may now run the marking batten through again making permanent marks.

6. Repeat the marking process on the top batten and strike the perp lines.

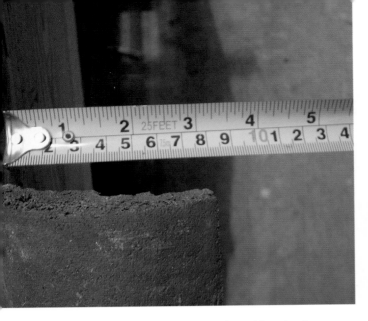

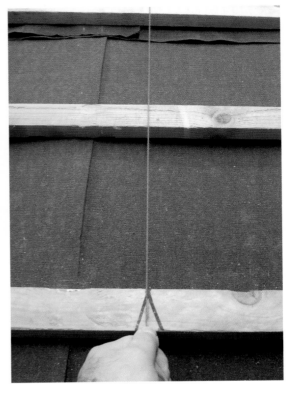

ABOVE: Measure the tile overhang (then divide by two).

RIGHT: Striking perpendicular lines.

BELOW: Set the permanent marks to the required overhangs.

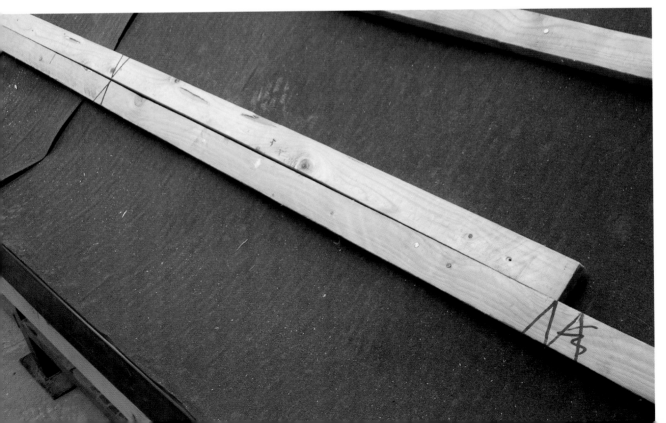

If the roof is slightly out at the top then your tiles will not be on the lines straightaway. You will have to open or close them until they are; from that point you will be laying them at the average gauge.

Remember only to use the shunt that the tile is willing to give you. This means that you must not force it open nor closed in a rush to get on the marks. Forcing tiles can make them twist, sit poorly and cause breakages.

VARIATIONS AND EXCEPTIONS

The setting out methods described thus far refer to the most commonly used roof tiles on the market today (for instance, concrete interlocking tiles, with two rolls and two pans). Rather than go through every type, the main differences that will affect your setting out are described here.

Left-Hand Verge Tiles

Some types of tile need to have the left-hand interlock removed (for instance, flat profiles) or have in their range a special tile that fits on the left-hand verge, sometimes referred to as left-hand 'finishers'. Left-hand verge tiles can vary in width compared with standard tiles so you should allow for this in any setting out that you do.

Flat Tiles

Flat interlocking tiles are normally laid at 'half-bond', like a slate or a plain tile, and so there is a little more work required in the marking out process. In simple terms, you need to mark the roof out twice, once for a full tile start and again for a half-tile start. By cutting the left-hand verge tiles and the 'handed' tiles provided (tiles supplied with a score line down the centre) you will have all the fittings you need for the marking out process.

Typical left-hand finishing tiles.

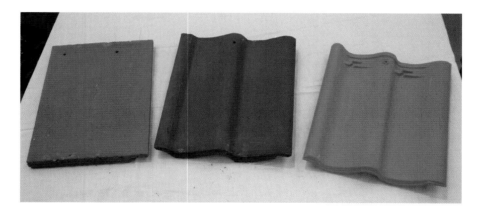

Handed tiles for 'half tile' starters and finishers.

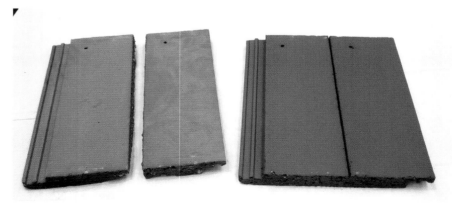

Marking out Roofs with Valleys

The drawings below show two roofs with valleys. The main difference between them is that on one the ridge lines are the same height and on the other they are not. This makes a difference in how the roofs are marked out.

We shall start with the roof with equal ridge lines. The elevations have been marked with letters to help the reader to understand the following setting out methods.

If we start with elevation A, the simplest way to mark out this roof is to start with a full tile mark on

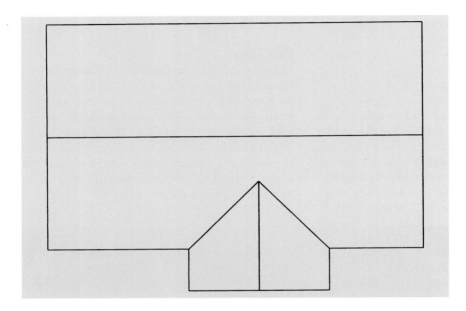

Typical roof with valleys and unequal ridge heights.

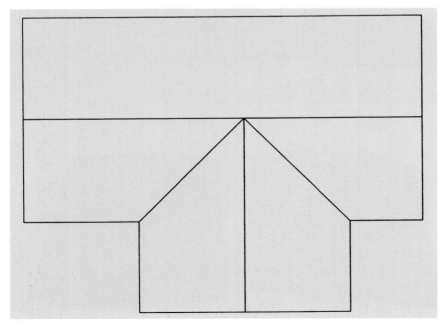

Typical roof with valleys and equal ridge heights.

*Elevations
marked A–E.*

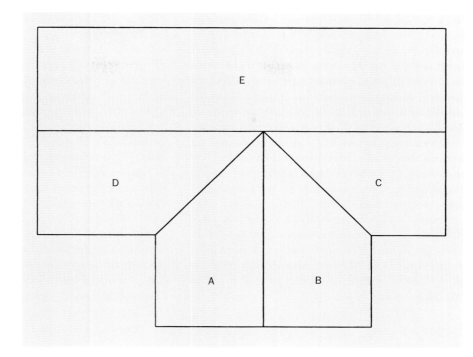

*Additional marks
in valleys.*

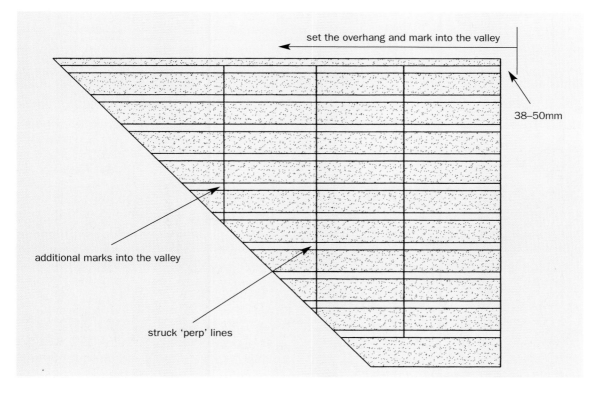

set the overhang and mark into the valley

38–50mm

additional marks into the valley

struck 'perp' lines

the right-hand verge so that the overhang is set between 38 and 50mm. With this as a starting point, transfer the marks from the marking lath to the top course batten and the eaves course batten and strike lines between the corresponding points. Additional marks, if required, can now be transferred into the middle to upper sections of the valley, if required, and lines struck from these points to the top course.

Elevation B is marked out from the left-hand verge inwards toward the valley. Extend the marking lath over the bargeboard at the same overhang as in elevation A and transfer the marks to the top and the bottom batten and strike lines between the corresponding points. On this side of the valley it is definitely advantageous to continue marking into the valley (as shown) because interlocking roof tiles are designed to be laid from right to left, and having extra marks provides more starting points for right to left tiling.

Elevation C is marked out in the same way as A, but the overhang needs to correspond with whatever has been worked out on the opposite (verge-to-verge) side of the roof (E). Elevation D is marked out in the same way as B, but again the overhang needs to correspond with whatever has been worked out on the opposite (verge-to-verge) side of the roof.

Where there are several courses above the valley, the top batten should be marked right through by using the required overhangs. The rest of the roof can be marked the same as described above, although many roofers prefer to use a second set of marks on the course immediately above the valley and the lines struck through. If you want to use the striking-through method, then there needs to be a decent distance between the two sets of marks. The closer they get together the more likely it is that the lines will be struck at an angle and therefore lose accuracy. Therefore, as a rule of thumb, there needs to be more

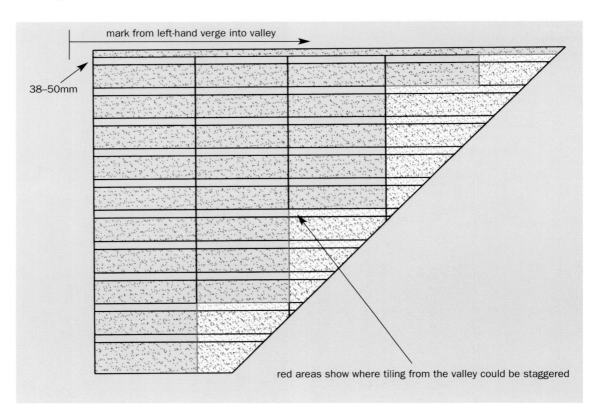

Tiling can be staggered to additional marks in the valley.

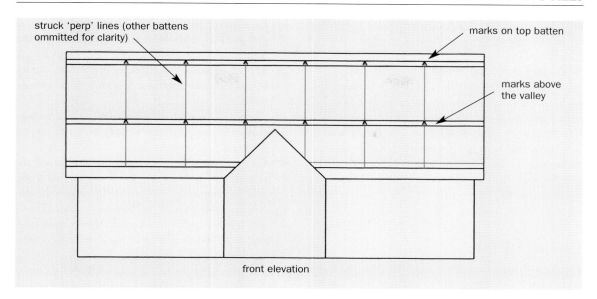

struck 'perp' lines (other battens ommitted for clarity)

marks on top batten

marks above the valley

front elevation

Striking through over minor valley sections.

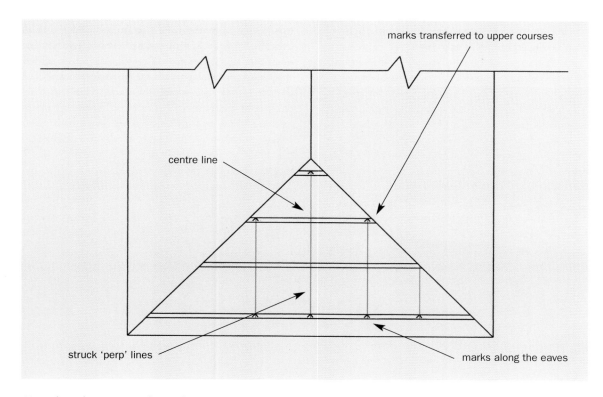

marks transferred to upper courses

centre line

struck 'perp' lines

marks along the eaves

Typical marking out to a hip end.

roof above the valley than below it, if you are going to strike through.

Marking out Hip Ends

Hip ends: many roofers do not bother marking hip ends out, but, for the couple of minutes it takes, it may make the job much simpler. Start by striking a line down the centre of the roof. The easiest way to find the centre is to use the central rafter as a guide. Next make a series of marks across the eaves (using a marking batten). The higher marks are made by moving the marking batten up the roof and striking through.

FIXING DETAILS

Laying Tiles

Perhaps the main selling point of interlocking tiles in comparison with slates and plain tiles (apart from the fact that they are cheaper) is the speed and ease at which they can be laid. Interlocking tiles are designed to be laid from right to left, and you will find it much quicker and easier if you stick to this method. The basic laying technique is as follows.

1. Positioning: place the first tile on the batten and pull it down to ensure that it is square on and the nibs are properly located.
2. Repeat with subsequent tiles laid from right to left so that they interlock accurately and without force.
3. Shunting: open or close the tiles in the direction they need to go in relation to your marks, do this gradually and without force.
4. Fixing: if the fixing specification indicates nail-only, then fix the tiles you have just laid; if the tiles are clipped and nailed, or clip-only, then you will probably have to fix the tiles one at a time as you lay them; clipping is much slower than nailing, so allow more time if the specification asks for this.

I have seen many so-called roofers tile row after row right across the roof and then walk all over the ones they have just laid; normally this means that the roofer cannot see the benefits of setting out or perhaps does not know how to do it. This is poor practice, which normally results in muddy footprints all over the roof, broken or cracked tiles (often hairline

First tile pulled down squarely on to the battens.

Lay tiles to marks without force.

Shunting the tiles open or closed.

Clipping and nailing.

cracks, which appear later) and is also actually a breach of health and safety regulations because tiles are classed as fragile and are not designed to be walked on, and, even if they were strong enough, there is still the risk of slipping. If you must be on the roof once the tiles have been laid, you should use a roof ladder or, if the specification allows for it, push tiles up on courses that are not nailed or clipped and use the exposed gaps as footholds.

Where possible, try to take the eaves course of tiles through first to check that your marks are correct and then tile up in columns of three to six tiles to the marks, starting with the right-hand verge, if applicable. This ensures that you are working off the battens and not the tiles; at least one foot (and normally one knee) should be on the battens at all times to avoid slipping and possible damage to the tiles. You should plan your work to ensure that you do not walk on the tiles once fixed; this is not always possible, but it is worth giving some thought to before you start.

Fixing Specifications

It is important that perimeter tiles (that is, eaves, verges, valleys, hips, top edges and abutments) are all mechanically fixed (nailed and/or clipped), according to the specification. The fixing specification for the main areas should be checked with the tile manufacturer's technical department. As stated in chapter 3, some of the main roof tile manufacturers now have an agreed Zonal Fixing Method, which has brought some degree of clarity to fixing specifications.

EAVES

Eaves Fillers and Clips

The purpose of eaves fillers is to close up any gaps under the tiles so that birds and vermin cannot enter the roof space. Flat-profiled tiles do not need fillers, but most medium- and deep-profile roof tiles do. The most common type of eaves filler is called a comb, for obvious reasons. These fillers normally come in different heights, so you should check with your merchant which one is right for the tiles you are using. The fillers are nailed along the edge of the fascia board, as shown. Where specified, install eaves clips appropriate to the type of tile you are using.

Typical comb-style eaves filler.

Short course under chimney.

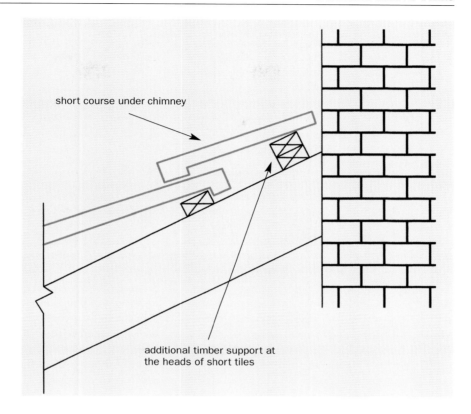

short course under chimney

additional timber support at
the heads of short tiles

CHIMNEYS

Below

When cutting to a chimney or some other penetration in the roof you will probably have to cut and fix the tiles. Below the penetration you should cut the heads off the tiles rather than the tails, and re-hole them with a drill. If the tile is less than about three-quarters of its original length then it is likely to need more support at the head, so check this before fixing the tiles and, if necessary, increase the thickness of the batten using additional timber (normally a double batten will do the trick).

Sides

When you are cutting to the sides of a chimney the cut should be as close as possible to the wall and at least half a tile wide; however, in reality there is little you can do about how the tiles fall so you can end up with small cuts. If the nail holes have been cut off you

will need to drill new ones and ensure that the tiles are securely fixed.

Back

If the tiles are too long to fit behind the chimney you have the choice of cutting something off the tails or of raising the batten behind the chimney slightly to pick them up a little. It is important not to get too tight behind the chimney (leave a gap of at least 100mm) since this can lead to blockages and water may then back up into the roof.

VERGES

Dry Verge

As with all proprietary systems, the manufacturer will provide a fixing guide with the materials, which must be adhered to. All the systems are designed to be quicker and easier to use than mortar bedding and, provided the instructions are followed, the installer should have few problems.

71

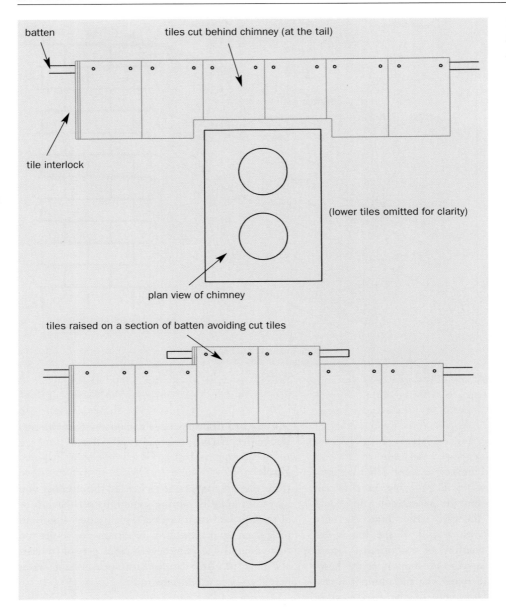

batten

tiles cut behind chimney (at the tail)

tile interlock

plan view of chimney

(lower tiles omitted for clarity)

tiles raised on a section of batten avoiding cut tiles

Bedding and Pointing

It is important to bed the mortar high enough so that the tile compresses it when it is placed. The general technique for bedding is to turn the mortar over several times with a trowel in a bucket or on a hand board so that it can be delivered in smooth and compacted shape. Start by bedding up a short run, say two or three tiles, to make sure that you are bedding to the right depth and, once you are sure, then continue to bed the rest of the verge. Note that the first tile may need more mortar than those that come after it because there is often a slight kick at the eaves. For deeper beds, packing material such as broken tiles should be used to reduce slump and shrinkage.

Typical dry verge in progress.

Bedding for first tile.

Mortar compacted when pressed by tiles.

Pointing to verge, general technique.

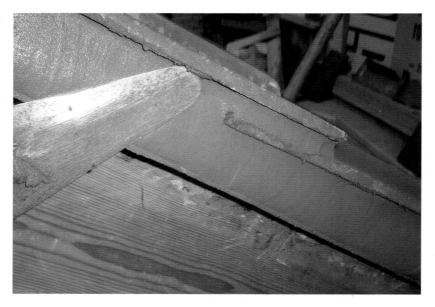

Shadow pointing.

Normally, if you try to point the verge straightaway the mortar will sag, so it is better to leave it to harden (go off) for a while and then come back to it. How long you should leave it depends on the depth of the bed, the weather conditions and how firm the mortar was to start with; but, in general, you should allow at least one hour, and you must ensure that bedding and pointing for verges or any other details are completed in the same day. Failure to do so may result in poor adhesion and the pointing may eventually crack and fall out.

The key to good verge pointing is to try and smooth the mortar out by using a steady, continuous motion with a slightly angled trowel (as shown). Normally, it is a good idea to use upwards strokes to prevent sagging.

Flush pointing or parging.

Pointing Styles

Styles of pointing may vary, depending on regional differences, client requirements or simply personal preference. Perhaps the most widely accepted style is to run the trowel just underneath the tiles at a slight angle to leave the edges of the tile clean. This is commonly known as 'shadow pointing'.

'Flush pointing' (or parging), on the other hand, covers the whole tile. This is perhaps the most common method of pointing because it is arguably quicker and easier to do than shadow pointing. However, the drawbacks with this method are that it tends to crack around the covered parts of the tile, especially around the interlocks, so it may be less aesthetically pleasing than shadow pointing.

'Brush pointing' is an old, traditional way of finishing the mortar in certain areas with extreme weather conditions. As the name suggests, the mortar is brushed to leave a textured finish, which is thought to be more durable and less prone to cracking than smooth pointing.

Tiling

A column of tiles not less than two tiles wide (normally to the first full perp line) should be taken all the way up the verge. From this point the tiles can be laid to the marks until the roof has been completed.

HIP AND RIDGE TILES

The information on bedding 'butt-jointed' ridge tiles and wet hips in this chapter (*see also* capped hip and ridge tiles) may appear to apply to interlocking tiled roofs only, but the general principles can be applied to plain tiles and natural slates as well. Therefore I have included most of the information on the subject here and, to avoid unnecessary repetition, I have covered any variations or additional information specific to the type of roof covering in the relevant chapters.

Before we look at the actual techniques of bedding ridge and hip tiles, there is one important piece of information that you should be aware of. Bedded tiles rely mainly on the tensile strength (that is, the resistance to breaking under tension) of mortar to keep them in place; but in some areas of the roof there is evidence to suggest that this cannot be fully relied upon. The areas in question are where the ridge tiles meet or pass over masonry, so, effectively, this means gable ends, party-walls and against chimneys or abutment walls. In these areas where different materials (masonry and timber) are in close proximity, differential movement can occur and it is this that can cause the mortar to crack and therefore separate from the ridge tile. If you notice, after any storm, where ridge tiles have become dislodged, it is almost always in these areas, and gable ends in particular because they are also the most exposed. Since September 1997 the guidance from the British Standards Institution has stated that in these areas, the end 900mm (two standard 450mm ridge tiles) of ridge tiling should be mechanically fixed (nailed or screwed, for instance) to provide the additional protection required.

Although this guidance has been around for several years, it is still far from common practice for it to be applied and not all specifications are explicit in requesting that it is carried out. Indeed, it is not until there is a roof failure that it normally becomes an issue, and even then only on certain types of contract where there is an inspection regime (for example, new build or local authority work). So, if you are intending to do any work that is likely to come under inspection then it may be wise to clarify the situation first. At the very least, you should consider some mode of fixing the end ridge tile, purely because it is such a vulnerable area.

BEDDED RIDGE TILES

General

Perhaps the most important thing to remember is to get the mortar consistency and strength right before you start. Remember, the mortar needs to be firm enough to support the ridge tile but wet enough to be workable and to create good adhesion with the roof tiles. The only real difference between bedding ridge tiles and hip tiles is that the former are significantly easier because you are bedding on to a consistent height, as opposed to a hip which has changing levels as you bed over cut tiles and overlaps.

One problem with bedding ridge tiles is that they have a tendency to wander if you bed them free-hand. This is not necessarily serious unless the line of the ridge is going to be overlooked, but, all the same, I would recommend inexperienced roofers strike lines on the tiles as you would on a hip. This will not only keep the ridge tiles straight, it will also ensure that sufficient lap is maintained (from ridge tile to roof tile) and provide a consistent guide for accurate bedding.

Keeping the ridge tiles level horizontally should be done by eye, not as you might think by spirit level.

However, you may, of course, use a straight edge if you feel that it helps. One of the main things is to retain a consistent bed height so that the ridge tile sits just slightly higher (say 10 to 15mm) than the required finishing position. If you can achieve this consistently it means that the amount of 'knocking-down' is kept to a minimum and levelling becomes much easier.

The basic technique for bedding 'butt-jointed' ridge tiles is as follows:

1. Position the first ridge tile so that it is central, with equal lap on to the tiles on both sides, and mark the edges with a trowel to provide the bedding lines (to mechanically fix the end ridge tiles you may need to install additional timber battens first – *see also* dry ridge for typical fixings).
2. Work the mortar in the bucket or on the hand board so that it is delivered in a neat, compacted shape, slightly inside the lines.
3. Place a full trowel of mortar at the end, press a piece of broken tile on to it and then bed on to this again so that the shape matches (and is slightly higher than) the ridge tile.
4. Knock the ridge tile down until the clearance (about 10mm) above the roof tiles is consistent on both sides; some roofers knock the ridge tiles right down to the surface of the roof tiles, but this

Marking and edge bedding the first ridge tile.

End bedding with packing.

Packing materials inserted into joints.

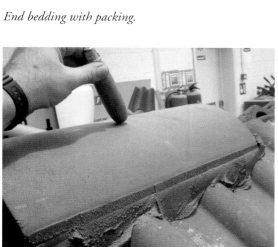

First ridge tile knocked down into position.

Mortar joints should be solid and even.

is a mistake because, if there are any slight lumps or bumps in the roof tiles, then they will show up in the ridge tiles; it may well be that the end ridge tile sweeps up slightly at the verge, this is often a result of the slight tilt caused by the insertion of an undercloak and is perfectly acceptable.

5. Once you are happy with the first ridge tile, insert a piece of broken tile in readiness for the next mortar joint; fill the mortar joint to a consistent width of about 12 to 15mm and place the edge bedding for the next ridge tile.

6. The next step is to position the ridge tile on to the bed and up to the edge of the mortar joint; you should find that one hand under the back of the ridge tile and the other at the side (near the front edge) will give you the control you need

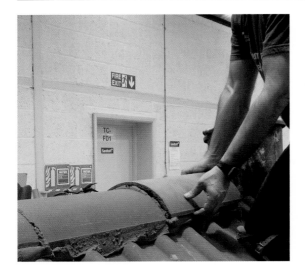

ABOVE: Pointing the joints.

TOP LEFT: Handling and placing subsequent ridge tiles.

LEFT: Pointing to the sides.

and will also help you to avoid trapping your fingers between the ridge tiles; push the ridge tile into the mortar joint and begin to knock it into place, you should alternate between knocking down and knocking across (into the joint) until you reach the desired position and the width of the joint has been squeezed to 10mm or less.

7. Creating this solid joint means that it should be much more durable and, as an added bonus, you will find it much quicker and easier to point; if you have done the joint correctly all you should

need to do now is to trim off the surplus mortar with a trowel and run the nose of the blade over it to finish it off; try to smooth the mortar up from either side and finish on top of the joint as this will hide any troublesome trowel marks.

8. To point the edges of the ridge tiles, first transfer any surplus mortar that has oozed out to areas where it is needed and add more if required, then smooth the mortar out with as few strokes as possible (that is, a continuous motion where possible) across the length of the ridge tile, but, if

the pointing is sagging slightly, use upwards strokes to correct it and, if this does not work, then you may need to leave it to go off slightly; another method is to press some small broken tile pieces into the bed to create more support; with regard to trowel techniques, some roofers use the front of the trowel and some the back, some use the same standard gauging trowel for bedding and pointing while others may have a smaller pointing trowel specifically for this task; this is really a matter of personal preference and, provided a smooth finish is achieved, then, by and large, anything goes.

Dry Ridge

As with all proprietary systems, the manufacturer will provide a fixing guide with the materials, which must be adhered to. While there are many different types of dry ridge available, they divide quite neatly into those which use an adhesive roll and those which use plastic rails. When using the former, it is important to make sure that the tiles are clean and dry so that the adhesive sticks properly. All the systems are

Small tile pieces at the hip should be mechanically fixed.

Typical adhesive roll-type dry ridge system.

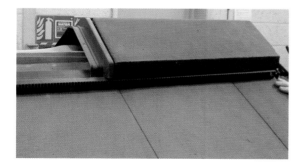

Typical interlocking rail-type dry ridge system.

designed to be quicker and easier to use than mortar bedding and, provided that the instructions are followed, the installer should have few problems.

HIPS

General

The cut tiles at the hip do not have to be particularly straight or neat, as in the valley, because they will be covered and so are not going to be seen. However, they should be cut close enough to the hip rafter to ensure at least 75mm of coverage when the hip tiles are laid. Many roof tilers hand-cut the tiles to the hips, but this is an acquired skill, which, while considered quicker by some, does have its drawbacks. For instance, hand-cutting produces more waste than machine-cutting because, in the latter case, the off-cut part of the tile may be used in the valleys (if applicable). Also, some corner-to-corner cuts are difficult to do, so time and tiles can be lost trying to overcome this, and hand-cutting can, if not done properly, leave hairline cracks in the tiles, which may open up when laying the tiles or at a later date. My advice for new and present roofers would be to abandon the idea of the hand-cutting of concrete interlocking tiles unless it is absolutely necessary and to cut interlocking tiles with a disc cutter.

While it is still fairly common practice to bed small pieces in place, mortar alone cannot be relied upon to hold them there. All cut tiles where the nibs have been cut off will need to be either clipped (clips are available from most tile manufacturers) or nailed in place. The latter may entail drilling, in which case I would recommend a 3 or 4mm masonry bit and a high voltage, cordless drill. You will probably need to introduce more fixing points; short off-cuts of batten are ideal for this.

In the case of a wet hip, it is important to remember to fix a hip iron in place (preferably before the underlay) at the eaves. This should be positioned approximately 50mm over the fascia board and fixed with two non-corrosive screws or large nails. Furthermore, the mortar for a wet hip needs to be quite firm, with a consistency similar to that of a very soft clay.

You will notice that I refer to hip tiles and ridge tiles as separate items and the reason for this is that, wherever possible, they should indeed be different from each other. As mentioned in chapter 2, the hip tiles should, wherever possible, be shallower than the ridge tiles. By using a hip tile, plus a steeper ridge tile, you will find that the resulting junction at the three-way mitre will be much more in line and also the hips will be slightly easier to lay because they tend not to sink as much when you are bedding them.

Typical dry hip system.

Dry Hips

Again, as with all proprietary systems, the manufacturer will provide a fixing guide, which should be followed. While there are many different types of dry hip about, they divide into those that use an adhesive roll and those that use plastic rails. When using the former it is important to make sure that the cut tiles at the hip are clean and dry so that the adhesive sticks properly. All the systems are designed to be quicker and easier to employ than mortar bedding and, provided that the instructions are followed, few problems should ensue.

Wet Hips (Butt-Jointed Hip Tiles)

If I had to ask a roofer to do one thing for me to prove that he could do the job, I would, without hesitation, ask him to bed and point a hip over some profiled tiles and finish off at the top with a three-way mitre (the junction at the top where two hips meet the ridge). While there are other roofing details that may look more difficult, most of these are knowledge- rather than skills-based. To put a hip up straight and true and to form a neat three-way mitre by using mortar is a true test of hand skills, which normally takes much practice and confidence. This, then, is something that is going truly to test the beginner, so if you are new to hips, always work to a line, make sure that the mortar is of the right consistency and take things slowly at first.

1. Assuming that all the tiles are cut and fixed in place; rest the bottom hip tile on to the hip iron so it is central and parallel to the hip rafter. Mark the sides of the hip tile with a pencil, and also mark where the bottom corners will need to be cut off.
2. Take a hip tile to the top of the hip and mark the edges, making sure that it is central and parallel to the hip rafter.
3. By using a chalk or redline, strike lines between the corresponding points. Note that when you come to bed inside the lines bear in mind that at least one should be kept visible at all times as a guide for keeping the hip straight. Which one you chose is a personal preference, but it is normally the side of the hip you are most comfortable on.

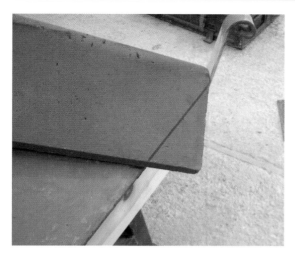

Placing and marking the first hip tile.

4. Cut the corners off the bottom hip tile and position the mortar just inside the lines. The bottom section should be solidly bedded with some tile packing to reduce shrinkage and cracking. Getting the correct bed height varies from one tile type to another and is just something that comes with experience, but, in general, you should bed higher than you expect to finish because hip tiles will normally sink a little, and it is much easier to knock a hip tile down than to lift it up. A little extra spot of mortar on either side on the back end of the bed where the end of the hip tile is expected to finish normally helps.

5. Position the first hip tile and gently knock it down into position so that one edge is to a line and it clears the tiles at the highest point (this will be where the tiles overlap) by about 10mm. Scrape off any surplus mortar that has oozed out

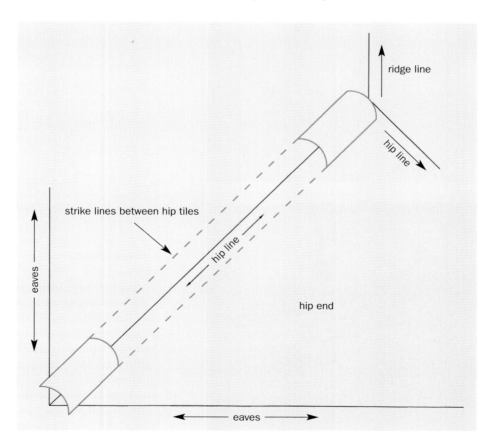

Striking lines for hip tiles.

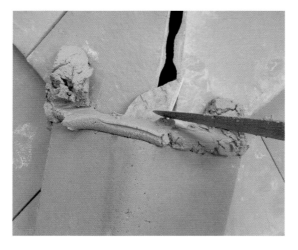

ABOVE: *Bedding for the first hip tile.*

TOP LEFT: *Positioning the first hip tile.*

MIDDLE: *Packing materials inserted into joints.*

BELOW LEFT: *Mortar joints should be solid without gaps.*

and transfer it to any areas that need to be filled.

6. At the first joint, insert a piece of broken tile (about the size of your palm) to act as support for the mortar joint. Bed the mortar joint solidly, evenly and without any noticeable gaps.

7. Bed and position the next hip tile, ensuring that the mortar joint is squeezed to leave gap of 10mm or less.

8. Continue bedding and positioning the hip tiles as described until you are within a couple of hip tiles of the apex. Keep to the line and knock the

ABOVE: Straightening the hip.

RIGHT: Bedding and positioning second hip tile.

hip tiles down into place so that the clearance above the tiles at the highest point (where two tiles overlap) remains consistent at around 10mm.

9. The next step is to ensure that the hip is straight when viewed from the side and from the front. First, position yourself at the bottom at the hip (in line with the hip iron) and look up it to find any obvious bends that need to be straightened out. If you have kept to the line, you might not have to make any adjustments and, if you do, they should be fairly minor. But, if any adjustments do need to be made, do them gently and gradually, preferably with someone else guiding you until the hip is straight. Normally this is done by tapping the offending hip tiles with the handle of your trowel or the rubber butt of a hammer. Having achieved this, move down the scaffold a few metres to view the hip from the side and look for any high spots. Tap the hip down and into line (again, gradually, with someone guiding if possible) using a wooden straight edge 2 to 3m long to check the alignment.

10. If there is a kick at the eaves then it is quite normal for the first ridge tile to tilt up slightly with the angle of the roof and, on a large sprocket, this may affect several of the bottom hip tiles. If this is the case, start levelling the hip once this break has finished taking effect.

Pointing

Once you are happy that the hip is straight you can point up the edges, the joints (*see also* ridge tiles) and the bottom edge where the hip iron is. Take care not to drop mortar on the tiles and ensure that you have a sound foothold on the roof wherever possible.

Using 'Ridge/Hip' Riders

'Riders' are brackets specifically designed to keep the hip (or ridge) straight both ways. They are simple to use and have become popular among many roofers, and, while some of those who learnt the 'by line' method (like me) might see the need for hip riders as

TOP: *Pointing the edges.*

MIDDLE: *Pointing the joints.*

BOTTOM: *Pointing the bottom of the hip.*

a sign of weakness, my advice would be to give them a try, especially if you are inexperienced in bedding wet hips.

Riders work by trapping lengths of straight timber runners (normally slate or tile battens) at the top and the bottom to form a channel for the hip tiles to sit in. The width of this channel can be adjusted to suit different hip tiles by loosening and retightening a hinge located at the top of the rider. Once the riders are in place on the hip then the hip tiles are bedded, as before, keeping the edges of the mortar set just inside (but never on to) the timber runners. The hip tiles are kept straight (as viewed from the front) by the channel that has been created by the riders and timber runners, and in line (as viewed from the side) by tapping the hip tiles down to the desired height as the hip progresses, using the upper edges of the timber runners as a guide. Once the hip is complete, the hinges are loosened and the timber runners taken gently out, at which point the hip is ready for pointing.

Three-Way Mitre

This is the junction where the top two hip tiles meet the first ridge tile. All three cut tiles should be made from full length tiles where possible, so the mortar has a good area to adhere to and the tile retains as much dead weight as possible. If a smaller cut is required as a fitter between the main hip tiles and the top 'cut' tile, then it should be positioned first before the three-way mitre is formed.

There are many opinions and formulae on how to cut three-way mitres, but some can appear quite complicated while others require the hips to have been laid perfectly for them to work. Human error can often throw these theoretical methods askew, so, in my own experience, I have found that it is often better just to use your eyes and judgement. The following simple method has served me quite well over the years:

1. Begin by positioning a piece of lead (code 3 will be sufficient) over the tiling at the junction of the three-way mitre; this is just insurance in case the mortar joints crack and allow water in at some point in the future.

2. Next, position the first hip tile to be cut so that it is in line with the existing hip tiles and, starting from the mid-point, mark a line from the centre of the ridge down to the edge of the hip tile. This is the first cut line. Now measure this distance; for most pitched roofs this normally should be about 175mm to 200mm.

3. From here, you take half the distance you have just measured (say 90mm) and mark this on the opposite side of the ridge. Then it is just a matter of joining up the points to mark the second cut line. The other hip tile may now be marked by using the same measurements on the opposite side of the tile.

4. Cut the two hip tiles for the three-way mitre and move them into position (dry) to check the accuracy of your cutting. It is at this point that you may need to make some adjustments (that is, cut one of the lines again) to at least one of the hip tiles. Once you are happy that the cut angles are correct and the hip tiles are pointing straight down the line of the hip, then you are ready to mark and cut the third part of the arrangement, the main ridge tile.

5. Position a ridge tile (dry) close to the hip tiles and mark cutting angles that will bring the tiles together. Cut the ridge tile and move it into position. The three-way mitre should fit snugly together, but, if it does not, then any adjustments should be fairly minor.

6. Finally, bed the three-way mitre in place by using good firm mortar and tile packing to support the tiles while you knock them down into the desired position. You may find that the ridge tile slants up slightly, but this is normal and quite acceptable, even if you have used different hip and ridge tiles.

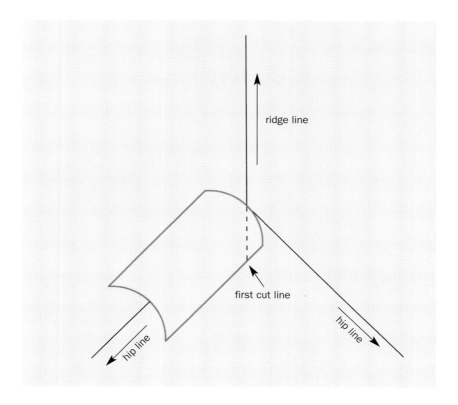

First mark for the three-way mitre.

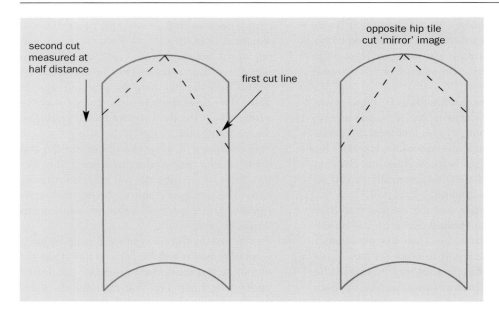

second cut
measured at
half distance

first cut line

opposite hip tile
cut 'mirror' image

*Cut lines
marked for
hip tiles.*

*BELOW: Cut lines
marked for the
ridge tile.*

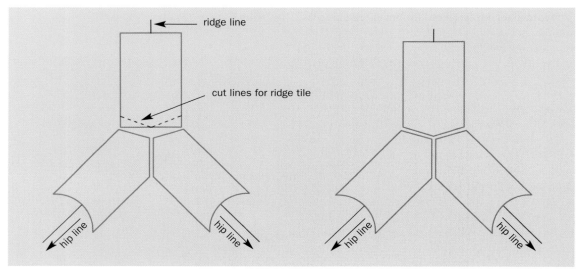

ridge line

cut lines for ridge tile

hip line

hip line

hip line

hip line

The 'Big-Top Effect' and How to Avoid It

Despite the fact that you can get separate hip and ridge tiles, many concrete interlocking tile jobs are done by using ridge tiles for both the hips and the main ridge. In fact, I would say that this has probably become the norm. The main problem with this is that the hips will always finish significantly higher than the incoming ridge. This is a combination of geometry and the fact that, on the hips, you are bedding over two thicknesses of tile (at the overlaps), while, at the ridge, there is only one thickness of tile; thus the hip line is at least 25mm higher than the ridge when using most concrete interlocking tiles. The result of all this is that the ridge tiles often need to sweep up significantly to complete the three-way mitre, an effect which looks not dissimilar to the sweep at the ends of a circus tent. Hence (at least in some parts) this has become known as the 'big-top' effect.

If you must use ridge tiles for the hips and the main ridge, then I have a tip, which was shown to me as an apprentice and it works very well, but you need to be aware of it right at the outset, and ideally before you start tiling. First, this method works well with segmental ridge tiles (that is, part-round), but less well with angled ridge tiles and so, if you are using the latter, you need to be aware that the resulting cuts could look a little odd. Secondly, if you are going to use this method, then you need to make sure that the tiling to the hips is cut close to the hip rafter so that there is still sufficient cover, because we are going to shift the hips off centre slightly.

The idea is that, before you strike your lines or set up your ridge/hip riders, you move both top marks in towards the centre of the hip end by approximately 25mm. What this does is lower the point at which the three tiles meet, and so the sweep from the ridge tiles is either taken out altogether or is at least minimized to an acceptable level. 'Rolling-in' the hips in this way will alter the cutting angles for the three-way mitre and it is likely that you will have to cut more by eye than by any formal method.

But, whichever method you use, it is worth pointing out that you do not necessarily have to wait until you get to the three-way mitre to start marking and cutting the hip/ridge tiles. There is nothing wrong with cutting them all first, positioning them and, once you are happy with the fit and the angles, setting your lines ridge/hip riders to them. In fact, this can work very well, especially when it comes to four-way mitres on pyramid roofs.

Capped Ridge and Hip Tiles

Capped ridge and hip tiles are edge-bedded and pointed just the same as butt-jointed ones, but are designed to overlap each at other with a cap, as the name suggests, so no mortar joint is needed

A completed three-way mitre.

Capped ridge/hip tiles.

between them. The cap is finished by applying a thin bed of mortar to provide a key and is then normally pointed up.

With a capped ridge you can, if you prefer, keep the hip straight by suspending a string line from the hip iron to the apex and use the spine of the tile to line it up. The first hip or ridge tile has the cap removed and it is considered good practice to turn the tile round so that the manufactured edge is seen and the cut edge is hidden.

VALLEYS

General

Tiles at the valley should be cut to the correct size and angle with a disc cutter and either bedded and mechanically fixed (that is, nailed or clipped) or installed to the manufacturer's instructions in the case of a dry valley. In some instances, where the tile

meets the raised channels at the sides of the valley liner, it may be necessary to remove one of the tile nibs to ensure that the tiles sit properly. If this is so, it is better to do it before cutting it because the tile is prone to break if it is done the other way around. Small cuts should be made from any breakages where possible to reduce waste and should always be mechanically fixed (nailed or clipped). Another excellent way to save tiles is to save and reuse the off cuts from the hips (if applicable).

Bedded Valleys

There are several ways of cutting and installing tiles to bedded valleys, some right, some wrong, and some downright dangerous. The right way is to mark each tile individually and then cut it on a level surface, such as the scaffold (remembering to take any nibs off first) and bed it in place, just as you would do at the verge. Some tiles may need 'rough' cutting

Bedding the valley.

Installing the first course.

first so that they can be fitted into the valley for marking.

This one-at-a-time method is probably the only way to ensure that the tiles are properly bedded in place (that is, so that the tile compresses the mortar). Most other methods rely on mortar being pushed in later on and are therefore incorrect on that basis alone. If tiles are bedded individually and the mortar is quite firm to start with, then you should be able to point the valley more or less straightaway. Use mainly upwards strokes to smooth the mortar out where it has squeezed out during bedding and transfer it to places where there are gaps. Add fresh mortar where it is needed and smooth out in short sections with mainly upwards strokes, taking care to keep the interlocks clear of mortar where two cut tiles meet. If the pointing continues to sag you may have to leave the mortar to stiffen for an hour or so before trying again; it may also be helpful to press home some small broken tile pieces for packing into the deeper beds. Always remember to clean down the valley after pointing.

The one-at-a-time method is, of course, quite slow and it can make it more difficult to get the valley straight, which is why many roofers lay the tiles straight in the valley, strike a line and cut the whole

TOP LEFT: *Working up the valley.*

LEFT: *Pointing the valley.*

Typical dry valley in progress.

thing in situ with a disc cutter. Often the rough-cut tiles are bedded in place, but this is largely ineffective because the vibration of the disc cutter often destroys any bond between mortar and tile. You should avoid using a disc cutter on a sloping surface at all costs because it is a highly dangerous practice and, in this situation, there is a real risk that the saw blade will go straight through the liner, which will then have to be patched or, worse still, the slit will be ignored or go unnoticed and the result will be a leaking roof.

On GRP valley liners the tiles are cut on to the sanded strip, which should be straight and consistent enough to work to, but you may find it more beneficial to strike your own line to work to instead. The finished channel should be approximately 125mm wide.

If you intend to use lead-lined valleys for interlocking tiles, then they will need an undercloak (about 50 to 75mm wide) fixed along each side to give the mortar something to key to. If this is not done then the mortar will crack and separate from the lead lining as it expands and contracts as the temperature changes. It is better to attach the undercloak with a suitable adhesive (such as a silicone-based, gun-applied adhesive) rather than by nailing because holes increase the risk of leaks.

Dry Valleys

As with all proprietary products, and as we have noted before, dry valleys need to be fixed to the individual manufacturer's instructions. In general though, it is important to ensure that each tile is either nailed or clipped and that small pieces are fixed and supported with the special valley clips or some other fixing provided.

CHAPTER 7

Plain Tiles

Plain tiles have been available in one form or another for hundreds of years and have proved to be an effective roof covering. At one time, when the range of materials was more limited, plain tiles were very common, but as new and cheaper tiles have entered the market (in particular, concrete interlocking tiles) their market share has gradually shrunk. Most plain tile work is now restricted to small works such as porches, bays and in vertical tiling, but they do appear on prestige developments, in conservation areas and on special curved and swept roofs where their small size makes them ideal. It should be remembered that the standard recommended (minimum) batten size for plain tiles is 38mm × 25mm for all rafter centres up to 600mm.

All the cutting in this chapter has been done deliberately with hand tools only to demonstrate the techniques involved. Disc cutters are marvellous machines, but they can break down (a classic instance occurs when pulling the cord out), and there are situations where disc cutting is not appropriate (as in the presence of hazards, dust and noise, for instance). In some situations hand cutting is actually quicker once you get used to it. When you hand-cut roof tiles, the edges will be slightly more jagged than the clean edge you get with a disc cutter (especially on concrete tiles), but viewed from ground level this is not normally an issue.

LEFT: First tile measured nib to tail.

RIGHT: Under-eave measured nib to tail.

SETTING OUT

Battens, Fixed Points and Gauges

Finding the First Fix Point

1. Turn the roof tile over and measure from the underside of the nib to the tail. Repeat this for the under-eaves tile and note both measurements (in this case 240 and 175mm, respectively).
2. Take your tape or rule and extend the end of it 50mm over the fascia board (or halfway into the gutter, whichever is smaller).
3. Mark the points at both ends of the roof and strike lines between them.
4. Fix the battens with the top edge to the line (just a few nails for the present, not driven).
5. The top edges of the battens are the first fixed points for the double course at eaves. Try a tile and an under-eaves tile on at each end to make sure that they overhang correctly and that the tails are in line before continuing.

The Maximum Gauge

The maximum gauge of a plain tile can be found in the trade literature or from the supplier's web site, but it is widely accepted as 100mm for pitched roofs; this is based on the formula:

[length − minimum headlap] ÷ 2 = maximum gauge
example: [265mm − 65mm] = 200mm ÷ 2 = 100mm

Battening Up

Unlike interlocking tiles, where you need to start working the gauge out almost immediately, the procedure with plain tiles is to batten the roof up at the maximum gauge and to make any the adjustments in the gauge in the last metre or so before you reach the ridge.

Finishing at the Ridge

At one time, most manufacturers of plain tiles used to produce special 'tops' tiles which were longer than a standard under-eaves tile. The extra length meant that the tops tile could be fixed to a batten above the last tile and retain the margin (100mm), and therefore the minimum headlap could be maintained. Now most manufacturers produce only one tile to do

Check that tiles are in line and overhang correctly.

both jobs (an eaves/tops tile) and this has led to some debate on how best to finish off at the top of the roof. When produced in clay, most eaves/tops still have just about enough hanging length to be fixed on a batten, but if you finish like this with concrete the eaves/tops tile is normally too short, so you may lose some of the headlap. On the other hand, if you simply hang the tops tile (as many do) then you maintain the minimum headlap, but you normally do so at the expense of a secure fixing. Some manufacturers do produce special clips which offer a solution to this problem although, in my experience, they are not commonly used nor available from most merchants.

So, is the solution to hang the tops tiles or fix them to a batten? Apart from contacting the manufacturer in the hope that he makes the special clips, this is one situation where the procedure to follow is not clear. Personally, I think that it is better to fix the tops tiles to a batten and to lose a few millimetres of headlap in what is a low-risk area to leaks rather than hang the tops loosely and rely on the ridge tiles to hold them on. Where possible, the batten used to fix the tops tile should be thicker (that is, deeper) than the other battens, so that it stands high enough for the nibs of the tops tiles to catch properly. You may find it handy to have some longer nails with you (normally 75mm

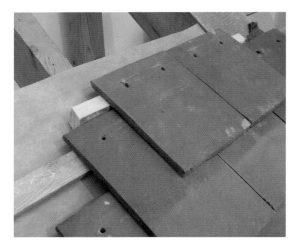

ABOVE: Typical pitch-finder in use.

TOP LEFT: Tops tiles 'hung'.

BELOW LEFT: Tops tiles fixed to batten on edge.

will suffice, but the actual length will depend on the depth of the timber you use) if you decide to finish in this way. The ideal size for a tops batten should be approximately 25mm wide and about 35mm deep. It is no wonder then, perhaps, that many roofers commit another small sin in the interest of common sense and use a batten on edge (technically, it is incorrect to nail across the grain in timber). To avoid splitting the timber, drill and screw the batten on edge or 'blunt' the nail heads by tapping them with a hammer before nailing them in. If you are going to use a batten on edge, install it tightly behind the last course of tiles after they are fixed in place.

But, whichever finish you have decided on, it is the top edge of the batten that carries the full tiles (not the tops) that gives you your fixed point at the ridge. You should make sure that the top batten is set down enough for the tiles, tops and a batten (if used) to fit in at the ridge with a few millimetres of clearance. Depending on the type of tiles you are using, the top batten normally finishes about 50mm down from the ridge for a 'hung' top and about 80mm down for a 'batten on edge' finish.

Dropping the Gauge at the Ridge
All you need to do to drop the gauge at the ridge is to

94

reduce the last few gauges as evenly as possible. You should restrict your adjustments to a maximum of 6mm to make sure that the drop in gauge is not too obvious. Normally there are several possibilities to choose from. For example, if you need to lose 30mm then you have the choice of dropping the last ten courses by 3mm each, the last five by 6mm each or the last six courses by 5mm each.

Battening for Hip and Valley Tiles

There is a range of hip and valley tiles (for instance, bonnet hips and purpose-made valley tiles) that are designed to carry the courses around from one side of the hip or valley to the other, and so it is important that the batten positions correspond on both sides. If the roof is of the same pitch on both sides, then there should be no problem with the battening, provided, of course, that it is marked and fixed accurately.

The easiest way to check the pitch is with a pitch finder, these may be obtained from most tile manufacturers, specialist merchants and now even large DIY stores. If there is a slight difference in pitch (up to 5 degrees) the batten positions can be brought into line by dropping the gauges evenly by a few millimetres each on the shallower (longer) side of the roof. If you do not have a pitch finder, then you can normally tell whether the roof is suitable by comparing the rafter lengths on either side of the hip or valley. Measure from the apex down to the eaves and, if they are within 5 per cent of each other (which equates to 50mm in 1m) then it is within 5 degrees.

The basic method for adjusting gauges where the pitch varies slightly is as follows:

1. Measure from the top edge of the first batten to the top fixed point on both sides of the roof and record the two measurements.
2. Work out the number of courses; this is dictated by shallowest/longest side (for example, if one side is 4500mm and the other 4350mm for a 100mm gauge there will be forty-five courses).
3. Next, divide the shorter measurement by the number of courses (thus, 4350mm ÷ 45 = 96.6mm)
4. Round up or down to the nearest millimetre (in this case 97mm) and, by using your tape or

rule, put this 'awkward' measurement on to a length of batten and mark off 97, 194, 291, 388, 485mm ...).
5. Batten the two roofs up at different gauges (100 and 97mm, respectively) but keep an eye on how the battens are lining up either side of the hip or valley. It is quite acceptable to adjust a gauge here and there as required, if you feel the need to do so.

Sometimes, when the pitch is not the same on the two sides, this means that one tile hangs down further than the other, causing a slight loss of alignment at the tails. If you are matching up the battens, this is unavoidable and the loss of alignment is often so small that it is not detectable from ground level. If you must line up the tails, this can be achieved by setting the battens slightly higher on one side of the roof than on the other.

With regard to the hip details, if the hip rafter is wide enough or there are noggins to secure the batten ends to, then begin by fixing a batten centrally down the hip rafter. This will not only provide a continuous fixing point for the hip tiles, it will also help to keep them straight. Cut the incoming batten ends to angle and butt them up to the side of the hip-batten. Make sure that each batten end is supported and nailed to either the hip rafter or a noggin.

It is now more common to find that you have neither a wide hip rafter nor noggins, so the only alternative is to cut the batten ends to an angle and nail them to the centre of the hip rafter. If you are faced with this situation, then you will need some longer nails (75mm or more) for fixing the hip tiles.

The valley detail is slightly different because of the area's vulnerability to leaks. The main thing to ensure is that the underlay is not punctured by the batten ends and that as few penetrations occur as is possible near the centre of the valley. It is probably wise therefore just to bring the batten ends straight into the valley but to stop them short by a few millimetres. If possible, get the joiner to include some noggins about 100 to 150mm back from the centre of the valley so that you can secure the batten ends properly.

TOP: Battens into the valley set back slightly to avoid punctures.

MIDDLE: Cutting in at the verges.

BOTTOM: Working out the overhang to a full or half-tile start.

Setting or Marking Out (Across the Roof)

General

Traditionally, plain tiled roofs were not marked out. The procedure for a standard verge-to-verge roof was to start at one end at a set overhang (say 50mm over), lay the tiles together without gaps and then make any adjustments to the other end by cutting the second or the third tile in from the verge.

If you use this traditional method rather than mark the roof out, be prepared to do a lot of cutting; a typical roof might be 5 or 6m long, which equates to fifty or sixty cuts on each side of the roof.

Overhangs

As with all slates and tiles, the undercloak for a plain tile roof should preferably extend between 38 and 50mm over the verge to comply with good practice guidance and the manufacturer's own technical information. It is rarely a problem with plain tiles to comply with this, and normally it can be achieved without cutting. What you are looking for is a situation where the tiles fall naturally over the verges at between 38 and 50mm. For small roofs, such as porches or lean-tos, just trying the tiles across will suffice. If a row of full tiles does not give you the overhang you are looking for, then try starting with a tile-and-a-half instead.

Normally, one of these two formations will produce the overhang you need or at least will come very close to it. You may need to space some of the tiles slightly to get the desired overhang; if this is the case do it evenly across a number of tiles (spacing with a trowel blade is recommended).

Marking-Out for Plain Tiles

Plain tiles may be marked out in much the same way as interlocking tiles, the only real difference is in how you make the marking lath. Remember that plain tiles are half-bonded so you will need a second set of marks. You can do this by going to any of the marks you have already made, marking a half-tile width to either side (normally tiles are 165mm wide, giving a half-bond of 83mm when rounded up) and then applying a second set of marks to the top and the bottom batten ready for striking.

Follow this method to create a marking lath for any plain roof tile:

1. Lay six tiles tightly together on any batten and mark both ends, leaving a small gap of (just a millimetre or two) at one end to avoid getting the tiles too tight. The idea is not to space the tiles, it is too lay them naturally without force while still allowing some room for movement or slight spacing later on if it is required.
2. Find a straight and fairly smooth batten (full length) and transfer the marks to the marking batten.
3. Cross out the part that is spare, to avoid confusion later on.

Fixing Details

Laying Tiles
The basic laying technique involves four stages.

1. Positioning – lay the tiles on the batten and pull or knock down to ensure that the nibs are properly located.
2. Shunting – open slightly or gently knock together the tiles in the direction they need to go in relation to your marks or to the verge; if it is small roof, do this gradually and without force.
3. Fixing – fixing is by double nailing to all perimeters and every fifth course as a minimum or as required by the specification.
4. Bonding – plain tiles lay broken bonded to the course below. In most cases this bond is created by starting every other course with a tile-and-a-half (creating a half-bond of approximately 82 or 83mm). In situations where it is not possible to retain a full half-bond the minimum sidelap for weathering purposes should not be less than 55mm.

Cutting Tiles (by Hand)
Unlike interlocking tiles, plain tiles (especially clay ones) are relatively easy to cut with hand tools. There are several methods of doing this and which one you use is a matter of your preference and, to some degree, of regional differences. In each case I would recommend that the tile is scored first with a scribe and that then any nibs which interfere with the cut are carefully removed with a hammer (always knock down, not up). From there you can either use a nibbler, pincers or two hammers.

ABOVE: Scribing the tiles.

BELOW: Nibbler in use.

Nibbler method: keep the jaws moving up and down at a steady, constant pace, bringing the tile through towards you as you cut, taking about 15 to 20mm off each time until you get to within about 10mm of the cut line. Sometimes, just as you are about to complete your perfectly straight cut, a small section will break off on the edge of the tile, often with the very last 'chomp' of the blades. Now, this can become frustrating, so to help in preventing this from happening it often pays to make sure to scribe a little deeper at the bottom edge of the tile and to trim to the corner before making the final cut.

If you are just cutting a tile to width (as opposed to a valley cut), then, if you take it off the right-hand side rather than the left, this means you will be cutting towards the top of the tile and, if a small corner does break off, then the tile can still be used because the blemish is covered by the next course. If you find that the nibbler is not cutting cleanly, the blades may need to be adjusted for height or to be changed if they have become worn.

Pincers: if you are using this method make sure the tile is scored a little deeper to increase your chances of success. It also helps to have strong hands. In reality, this is just a matter of snapping off pieces of the tile, larger ones at first and smaller ones as you get nearer to the cut line.

Eaves

When using plain tiles there should always be a double course at the eaves; this consists of full tiles laid at half-bond over the shorter, under-eaves tiles. If you start with full-width under-eaves, then your next course up will start with a tile-and-a-half; if you start with half an under-eaves (or tile-and-a-half down to size), then the next course will start with a full tile. If you are working towards a verge, try the last few tiles

LEFT: Cutting into the corners.

BOTTOM LEFT: Laying and fixing the under-eaves.

BELOW: Laying and fixing the first course.

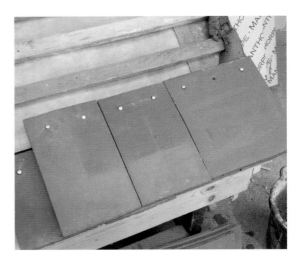

through to the end, just in case they need to be spaced out slightly. I would recommend that you take the double course at the eaves all the way through to check that everything fits before tiling the rest of the roof. Note that in some cases it may be acceptable to dispense with the under-eaves tiles provided that an appropriate plastic eaves course (similar to felt support trays) is installed in their place and that this has been agreed beforehand.

Verges

Plain tile verges are formed by laying tiles and tiles-and-a-half on alternate courses normally, with at least one or two tiles next to them for stability. The key to good plain tile verges is in the mortar work. The pointing method shown here is the traditional way to finish a plain tile verge and is known in some parts as 'herring bone' pointing because it resembles a fish bone when completed. Flush pointing or 'parging' on plain tiles should be avoided because, unless it is a style specific to a region, it ruins what could have been an attractive roofing feature. Follow this method and, with a little care and practice, you will soon master this traditional skill.

1. Begin by bedding up the verge so that the bed is high enough to be compressed by the tiles when laid.

Bedding the under-eaves.

Bedding the first course.

2. Run the blade of the trowel along the verge mortar at a slight angle so that the edge of the under-cloak is visible; this will help to keep the verge straight when tiling.

3. Press the first under-eaves tile into place so that it is straight with the verge and is pulled down square on to the batten. Lay several more under-eaves next to it and double-nail them all. Carefully place a thin bed of mortar on top of the first under-eaves tile, making sure that the mortar dies away near the tail.

4. Press the first tile (or tile-and-a-half) into place and check that it is straight with the verge and is pulled down square on to the batten. Lay several tiles next to this and double-nail them all.

5. Cut a long, triangle-shaped bed of mortar (about 25mm wide to almost nothing) and place this on to the first tile, as shown. If you are using a standard gauging trowel, the distance from the back edge of the trowel to the part where it starts to curve is a good guide for the length of bed required. Double-nail the verge tile and lay three or four tiles next to it.

6. From here repeat the process, alternating with tiles and tiles-and-a-half on every other course. Keep an eye on the mortar to make sure that it is being compressed, and, if it is not, then add some height where needed. Also, keep an eye on the

mortar that is oozing out too much when you press the verge tiles; trim this off with the trowel as you go to avoid its staining the tile edges. Double nail all perimeter tiles plus every fifth course as a minimum or greater if the specification requires it.

7. At the top of the verge, the end tops tiles will be either a full tile or a half. If it does finish with a half then you have a choice of cutting an eaves/top in half or cutting a tile-and-a-half down

ABOVE: Progression up the verge.

BELOW: Pointing to plain tile verge.

to size. The former retains the proper machine edge finish, while the latter gives a little more stability, but you are normally left with an unsightly cut. Both methods are acceptable, but, given the choice, I would tend to go with the half tile, especially for low-level work which will be seen.

8. Pointing the verge is easy if you have bedded it correctly. The verge should be full of slightly compacted mortar with few (if any) gaps and with minimal (if any) mortar stains on the tile edges. If you need to add mortar, do so carefully and in small amounts so as not to stain the tiles. Simply run the trowel underneath the edges of the tiles at a slight angle (2 or 3mm) in a steady, upwards motion, slowing slightly to move up and behind head of the next course. Periodically, stop to point between the tiles by running the blade down at a slight angle from the head of the tiles down to the tails.

Chimneys and Abutments

Below

Where possible, try to finish as you would at the ridge (that is, with a topper), but, if the tiles do not fit in below the penetration and you need to cut them, do so at the heads, not the tails, and re-hole them with a drill.

Sides

When you are cutting to the sides of a chimney or an abutment in plain tiles, make sure that you have some tiles-and-a-half available to avoid small cuts. The basic procedure is to lay the tile (or tile-and-a-half) you need to cut one tile back from the wall, overlap it with a full tile and mark the cut. Once cut, switch the cut tile and the full tile around to leave a tight, neat finish against the wall. This switching technique is one that can also be used at other details covered later in this chapter, such as bonnet hips, purpose-made valley tiles and vertical angle tiles.

Soakers

Although not all roofers do their own lead work (the work is shared between plumbers, lead workers and roofers who tend to do more re-roofing work than new build), all roofers should at least know how to cut and install soakers. These are small, rectangular flashings, normally made from code 3 lead, which sit between each course of tiles where they come to a wall.

The length of a soaker is determined by adding the gauge to the headlap, plus 25mm. For plain tiles this means the soaker needs to be 190mm (100 + 65 + 25) in length for pitched roofs and 175mm (113.5 + 37.5 + 25) for vertical tiling. The width should be 175mm, with the soaker folded at right angles to give an upstand of 75mm and a lap on to the tiles of 100mm.

The correct way to install a soaker is to place it on top of the tile and bend the top 25mm over to form a nib, which sits over the back of the batten. Normally, the bottom edge of the soaker is set a few millimetres up from the bottom edge of the tiles to avoid lifting them and so that the lead is not seen. If the detail starts with an under-eaves tile, then this should be

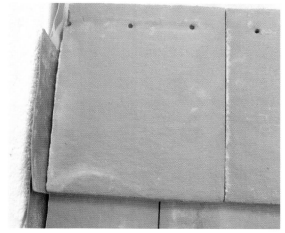

TOP: Marking the cut tiles (or tile-and-a-half).

MIDDLE: Switching the tiles – cut edge now tight to abutment.

BOTTOM RIGHT: First course installed over soaker.

BELOW: Soakers installed to under-eaves course.

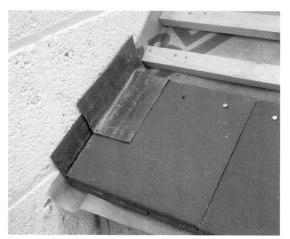

fixed first before the soaker. This first soaker will need to be slightly longer to cover the under-eaves tile plus the 25mm-fold at the top edge (normally 225–235mm).

Back

As you have a course of tiles every 100mm, this is usually just a case of deciding which is the most suitable to carry the tiles behind the chimney. What you are looking for is a course that gives you sufficient lap on to the back gutter lead flashing (*see* chapter 10), while still leaving a decent gap behind the chimney so that blockages are avoided. This section should be treated like the eaves, so you will still need a course of under-eaves tiles.

Bedded Ridge and Hip Tiles

There is nothing really to add on installing ridge and hip tiles that was not covered in the previous chapter, other than to say that ridging on to plain tiles is actually much easier because you do not get the rolls and pans associated with most interlocking tiles; the surface is flat, and so the bedding and pointing are straightforward.

Bonnet Hips

To begin, position the bonnet hip tile in the approximate position where it will eventually be fixed and mark the seams with a pencil.

Fix the under-eaves tiles in place so that they provide at least 55mm of sidelap to the bonnet, and use a wide tile (a tile-and-a-half cut down to size or a tile on edge) to cut into the centre of the hip. If a tile on edge is used, take the nibs off first and drill new nail holes for the fixings. It may be necessary to round off the tips of the tiles if they are not quite long enough to form a full mitre. If sidelap or nail holes are still of concern, then apply a code 3 lead soaker across the affected area.

TOP: Soaker installation in progress.

MIDDLE: Traditional clay-capped hip/ridge tiles.

BOTTOM: Marking the seam positions for the first hip tile.

Under-eaves cut to mitre.

Use of soaker to protect joints and nail holes.

1. Once the eaves course has been established, lay a full tile on the first course on either side of the hip. Lay a tile next to them to make sure that they are square and pulled down on to the battens. You may need to take the top corners of the tiles off for them to avoid their clashing at the hip.
2. Position the first bonnet hip tile over the tiles, making sure that it is central to the hip and the bottom edges are in line with the corners of the

tiles. Run a pencil down either side of the bonnet to leave cut marks on the tiles.
3. Cut the tiles and reposition them and the bonnet hip tile to check for accuracy.
4. Once you are happy with the cuts and the alignment of the bonnet, then take the bonnet off and place a bed of mortar underneath it, taking care not to get any in the seams of the tiles. It is normally a good idea to insert one or more tile slips to cover the open joint at the eaves and to act as a

Marking the tiles for the first bonnet hip tile.

Checking the cuts 'dry' for accuracy.

103

Bedding the first bonnet.

Fixing the first bonnet and adjacent tiles.

bridge for a second bed of mortar. The shape of the bed is quite important; try to copy the shape of the bonnet and, as always, put enough in so it compresses when the tile is laid.

5. Nail the first bonnet hip tile and the tiles adjacent to it. Fix several under-eaves and full tiles on both sides of the hip.

6. Set the next course of tiles to half-bond and tile back into the hip from both sides. Position and

cut tiles (or tiles-and-a-half, if the gap has widened) to fit between the last full tile and the bonnets, using the same method as before with the first course. Mark on where the bonnet will come to before bedding it slightly back from the line and nailing it in place, always checking that it is central and is in line with the bottom corners of the tiles.

7. Depending on the pitch of the roof, the cut tile

Courses set at half-bond and tiled back into the hip.

Setting and marking the bonnets.

104

'fitter' that sits next to the bonnets may vary in size as the hip progresses. Where necessary, use tiles-and-a-half to avoid small cuts. In general, it is not a good idea to let the cut tiles become smaller than 125mm wide and, in some cases, this means that two cuts may be needed. If you do have to double-cut then, for bonding purposes and aesthetic reasons, it is normally better to keep the cuts a similar size. The important factor is that the minimum sidelap does not fall below 55mm.

8. Carry on bedding and fixing the bonnets all the way to the top of the hip. The last bonnets, which fall on the tops course, may need to be cut at the head and drilled to create a new nail hole. The junction at the apex may get a little cramped, so you may need to improvise with regards to cutting tiles and bonnets and use soakers on any joints where sidelap has been lost.

9. Point the bonnets carefully to leave the edges clean of mortar.

Arris Hips

Arris hip tiles are similar to bonnets but are more angled and are designed to fit close to the tiles so that you do not have to bed and point them. They are available for several different roof pitches and if you get the right ones there should be no need to cut the tiles at the sides. In clay, arris hip tiles are normally available at 35, 40, 45 and 50 degrees and in concrete at 35 and 40 degrees only.

If for any reason you are losing or gaining sidelap and need to cut the adjacent tiles then follow the method described in the section on bonnet hips.

You may find that, if there is a sprocket or slight kick at the eaves, then this alters the pitch of the roof in the lower courses and so there may be some angled cutting to do on the adjacent tiles until you are on the roof pitch proper.

TOP: Bonnets in progress.

MIDDLE: Pointing to bonnet hips.

BOTTOM: Arris hip tiles.

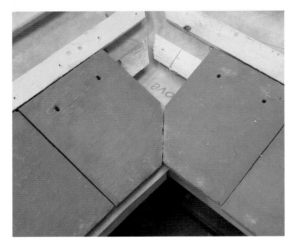

TOP: *Marking the first under-eaves tile for purpose-made valley tiles.*

MIDDLE: *Cutting and placing the mitred under-eaves.*

BOTTOM: *Checking the first valley tile for sidelap.*

Valleys

Purpose-Made Valley Tiles (Concrete)

In concrete, valley tiles are normally available in just one 'universal' fitting, so, unless you are very fortunate, you will have to cut the adjacent tiles to fit and will lose or gain sidelap on each course. To maintain the minimal sidelap you cut tiles or tiles-and-a-half down, while avoiding narrow cuts (minimum cut size 125mm), exactly the same as for bonnet hips.

1. To begin, position one of the under-eaves tiles into the valley and slide it along until it can go no further. Make a mark from the centre of the valley through to the bottom edge of the under-eaves tile. After cutting this tile, turn it over and use it as a template to mark the opposite under-eaves tile; cut this as well and nail them into place. Check that there is at least 55mm sidelap either side of the valley tile and make any amendments before continuing.

2. Once the under-eaves course has been established, take off the purpose-made valley tile and lay two full tiles on both sides, making sure they are pulled down squarely on to the battens. Position the first valley tile over the tiles, making sure that it is central to the valley and the bottom edges are in line with the corners of the tiles. Assuming that the roof pitch is equal on both sides, the cutting angle (if any) should be about the same each side. Score down either side of the valley tile with the scribe to leave cut marks on the tiles below.

3. Cut the tiles and reposition them alongside the valley tile to check for accuracy. Once you are happy with this, nail the adjacent tiles. Fix several under-eaves and full tiles on both sides of the

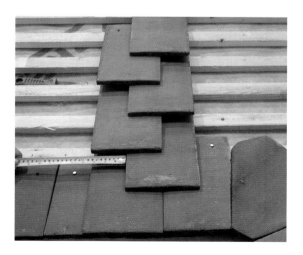

TOP LEFT: Position full tiles for first course.

TOP RIGHT: Scribing the tiles.

MIDDLE LEFT: Checking the cutting angles.

MIDDLE RIGHT: Fixing the first course.

BOTTOM RIGHT: Setting the next course to half-bond.

Tiling back into the valley.

Purpose-made valley in progress.

valley. Note that there are no nail holes in the valley tiles, this is deliberate to avoid leaks so do not be tempted to drill and fix them.

4. Set the next course of tiles to half-bond and tile back into the valley from both sides. Position and cut tiles or tiles-and-a-half to fit between the last full tile and the valley tile, using the same method as for the first course. Always check that the valley tile is central and is in line with the bottom corners of the tiles. Continue up the valley marking, cutting and fitting the tiles in the same way for subsequent courses.

Depending on the pitch of the roof, the cut tile 'fitter' may vary in size as the valley progresses. If the gap grows then use tiles-and-a-half, if it gets smaller continue cutting out of a full tile but keep an eye on the sidelap in relation to the valley tile as the fitting tile narrows. In general, it is not a good idea to let the cut tiles get smaller than 125mm, and so, where the gap from tiles to valley tile leaves a cut smaller than this, you may need to trim something off the next tile back as well.

Purpose-Made Valley Tiles (Clay)

In clay, purpose-made valley tiles are normally available at 35, 40, 45 and 50 degrees. If you can get the right ones for the roof pitch you are working on, or

are prepared to pay for them to be made, then they should give you half-bond and there should be no cutting to do at the sides. If, for any reason, you are losing some sidelap and need to cut the adjacent tiles, then follow the method described in the previous section.

You may find that, if there is a sprocket or slight kick at the eaves, this alters the pitch of the roof in the lower courses and so there may be some angled cutting to do on the adjacent tiles until you are on the roof pitch proper.

Open or 'Cut' Valleys

The correct formation for a lead-lined valley requires that the valley boards are installed to the same level as the rafters. This involves cutting and dropping the valley boards down between the rafters on noggins, and it may also be necessary to top this off with 6mm plywood boards to ensure a smooth base for the lead. The tilting fillet is then installed to the same height as the incoming battens so that the edges of the cut tiles are supported (*see* the picture on page 39).

There is a significant amount of work in forming this detail properly, so expect to find that the valley boards are fixed straight on top of the rafters. When this became common practice I am not sure, perhaps it always has been so, but what I do know is that, although it might be technically incorrect, the vast majority of valleys I have seen were and still are formed with the boards on top. When the boards are on top the code 4 or 5 lead lining is just welted (folded) inwards at the edges by about 25mm, with the tiling carried over the welted edge by about 50mm.

Whether using a lead-lined valley or a pre-formed GRP valley liner, it should be noted that plain tile valleys should not be blocked with mortar (that is, pointed) on their cut edges. Plain tiles shed water by allowing it in at the seams and then disbursing it via the tile underneath. Blocking the ends with mortar can trap the water in the roof, allowing it to back up and enter the roof space. I think this poor practice has crept in from interlocking tiling; often people ask for it because they think that all valleys need to be pointed, but this is a mistake. Open valleys in plain tiles have been formed quite successfully without any mortar for a great many years, but, if you must use mortar, make sure the tiles are just back bedded, well away from the cut edges.

Plain tiles should not be cut to a point in the valley, which means that they must retain some width at the tail (as much as possible, but in practice no less than 25mm). The cut line should extend well above the margin to ensure the correct lap on to the valley liner and to maintain the sidelap on the course above.

Where necessary, use tiles-and-a-half to avoid small cuts or to extend the head of the tile further into valley.

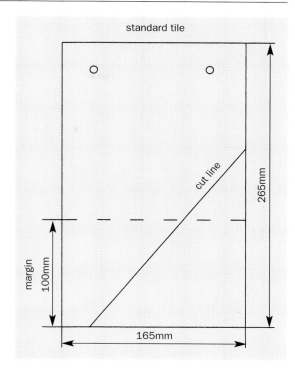

ABOVE: Cut tiles should retain some tail width and end well above the margin.

BELOW: Tiles-and-a-half used to avoid small pieces and extend into valleys.

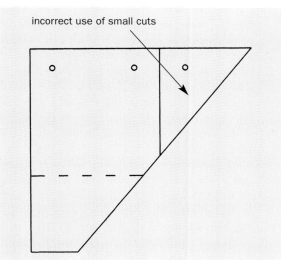

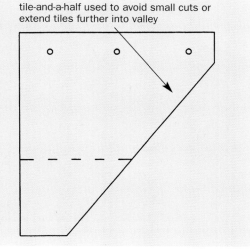

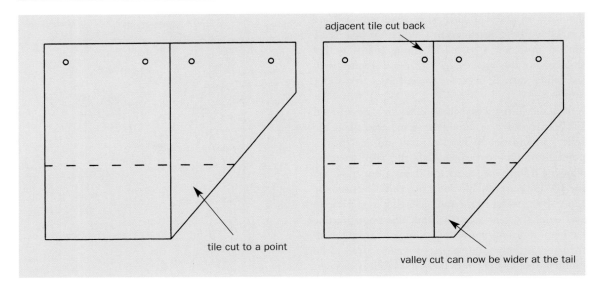

adjacent tile cut back

tile cut to a point

valley cut can now be wider at the tail

Adjacent tile cut back to retain tail width.

At times, you may be faced with a situation where a tile-and-a-half is not quite wide enough, but the alternative is a tile cut to a point. The way around this is to trim back the next tile sufficiently so that the valley cut is no longer to a point.

The conventional method for tiling an open valley in plain tiles is:

Installing the under-eaves.

1. Strike or mark a line on the valley liner where you want the tiles to be cut to. Normally this is a minimum of 50mm over the edge of the tilt fillet for a lead-lined valley, and about the same for GRP valley liners. Begin by marking and cutting the first under-eaves tile to the line and lay two or three more next to it. Double nail the under-eaves.

2. Lay the first course of tiles so that they are at half bond with the under-eaves and mark the first tile or tile-and-a-half in the valley along the cut line.

3. Cut and nail the tile in place, and set further courses to half bond. (Note that, if the valley is lead-lined with the boards on top of the rafters, you may need to take the tile nibs off where they fall on the lead to help them to sit properly. If this is the case, take the nibs off before cutting the tiles.)

4. Continue to set each course at half-bond to the one below and tile back into the valley, cutting the tiles and/or tiles-and-a-half to the line. Instead of marking exactly to the line, try marking from the line at the top part of the tile to a point about 3 to 5mm back on to the tile below. This might look a little odd up close, but is a

ABOVE: Marking the first valley cut.

ABOVE RIGHT: Installing the first cut and setting tiles to half-bond.

MIDDLE: Marking and cutting tiles (slightly on to the tile below).

BOTTOM: Open valley in progress (note how tiles line up).

good way to keep the valley looking dead straight when viewed from a normal angle.

Vertical Tiling

The first thing to say about vertical tiling is that you do not need as much headlap and you can therefore increase the battening gauge if you wish. The maximum gauge for vertical plain tiling is either 114mm or, more commonly, 115mm, depending on the manufacturer. The only real significance of the greater gauge is that you need fewer courses to do the job, and therefore fewer tiles.

Bottom Edges

When tiling above an opening window, check that the tiles do not catch and, if they do, then reduce the overhang. In pitched roofing the tiles normally need to extend 50mm over the fascia board so that water

Traditional-shaped flashing under sill.

External angle tiles, bottom course.

runs into the gutter properly, but in vertical tiling you only need about 25mm to form a drip (an edge that water gathers on and drops from).

Top Edges

How you finish at the top edge depends on whether or not you need to protect the topper course from water ingress or not. If the top course falls below a window frame, then you need a lead flashing (which should preferably be installed before the window). Traditionally, the lead is cut to a pattern and in many cases painted as well.

If the top edge is protected by a deep, overhanging soffit, the chances of water ingress are very low so you could probably do without a flashing, unless, of course, you want to for aesthetic reasons.

Internal and External Angles

These fittings come left- and right-handed with two holes on one side and one on the other, but are normally nibless. To start off, mark the edges of the first angle tile and proceed to install the under-eaves at half-bond.

From here it just a case of fitting left- and right-handed fittings on alternate courses and the adjacent tiles. All fittings and tiles must be twice nailed. If there is a kick at the bottom edge this will make the angle for one or more courses more shallow, so you may need to cut some of the tiles adjacent to the fittings to a slight angle for a better fit.

If you need to cut a vertical angle tile down to match in with the topper course, cut the top of the tile off rather than the bottom, and drill new fixing points.

If you are tiling to another internal or external angle then you mark and cut the tiles adjacent to the fittings, similarly to the way you would to a wall (*see* chimneys and abutments covered earlier in this chapter).

Gable End Details

Winchester Cut
The first thing to note is that Winchester cuts are not recommended where the roof pitch above the gable end is less than 40 degrees. This style of finish involves the angled cutting of tiles-and-a-half and the adjacent tiles at the end of each course (to create a 50p-piece like effect). The process starts by cutting a tile-and-half from one of the bottom corners to a point approximately 100mm wide at the head, so that at least one nail hole is retained. Take this to the appropriate end of the roof and position a full tile loosely on one of the battens, overhang the cut-tile-

ABOVE: *External angles tiles in progress.*

BELOW: *Establishing the templates for a Winchester cut.*

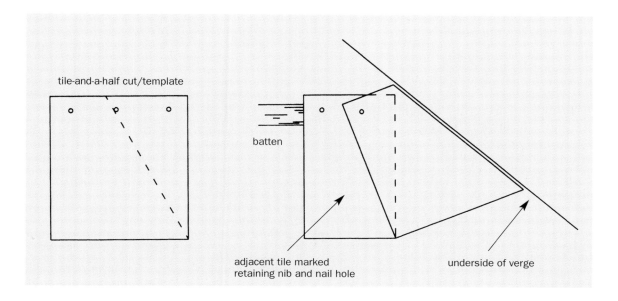

tile-and-a-half cut/template

batten

adjacent tile marked retaining nib and nail hole

underside of verge

and-a-half and mark the tile. It is important that at least one nail hole and one nib are retained for this second cut.

Winchester cut in progress.

If you are happy with the size and the angle of the cuts then mark the tile-and-a-half with a 'T' for template and use it to mark cuts for both sides, turning over the template to mark those for the opposite end.

The best way to start tiling is to strike a line down the centre of the gable end (on to the battens) and work away from it so that you are creating on one side a mirror image of the other. As you approach the end of each course, mark and cut the tiles (or tiles-and-a-half) with a template and nail all the tiles in place. While the minimum sidelap for vertical tiling is still 55mm, as it is for pitched roofs, in practice this is sometimes difficult to adhere to on a Winchester cut. However, you should avoid any straight seams (one in line with the other directly above) and try to ensure that there is as much sidelap as possible, even if this means taking a course back off and re-cutting it to suit the next one.

Sussex Cut (Soldier Course)

This detail is used on gable ends where the roof pitch is too shallow to take a Winchester cut. To form this detail fix two or more raking (that is, at an angle) battens to run parallel to the underside of the verge before you being tiling. The top corners of the main tiles or tiles-and-a-halfs are cut to the underside of the raking battens before being covered.

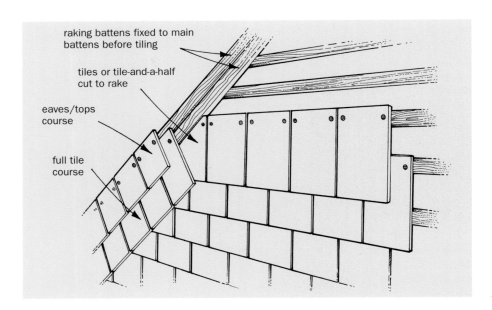

raking battens fixed to main battens before tiling

tiles or tile-and-a-half cut to rake

eaves/tops course

full tile course

'Sussex' cut or soldier course.

CHAPTER 8

Natural Slates (Regular Sized, Centre Nailed)

SETTING OUT

Working out the Gauge (Going Metric)

Slate gauges are worked out by taking the minimum headlap away from the full length of the slate and then halving the resulting number. The headlap for slates varies depending on several factors, including the roof pitch, the location and the level of exposure to driving rain, so you should always check this with the supplier if you are in any doubt. Traditionally, British slates have always been supplied in, and therefore worked in, imperial measurements and the 'default' headlap of 3in (unless otherwise stated) made the mathematics simple. For an 18in-slate, you took 3in off for the headlap to give you 15in, and half of that is obviously 7½in. All slate gauges, it seemed, would work out to a full or a half inch, so roofers were happy, and to this day most roofers of a certain age will continue to use imperial.

One problem with imperial measurements is that they do not always convert well into metric, and the fact is that the vast majority of slates are now imported (mostly from Spain) and they are in round metric measurements, such as 350, 400 and 450mm. For a 400mm-slate with a standard 76mm headlap, this means taking 76mm off to give you 324mm, and half that is 162mm. Most slates are now supplied pre-holed, so you need to ask what headlap they were holed for so that you can get the right gauge. To make gauges easier, 80mm is often used instead of 76 for the headlap, so the previous example would read 400mm, less 80mm equals 320mm, so half that would give you 160mm.

Battens, Fixed Points and Gauge Adjustments

At the Eaves

The top edge of the first batten should be set so that the head of the first full slate sits at least halfway on to it when laid, with the tail extending halfway into the gutter (typically 50mm over the fascia). The next batten is set one gauge down for the under-eaves slates. The holes for an under-eaves slate fall quite near the top edge of the slate and this may result in its breaking above the hole during nailing. One way to prevent this is to position an additional batten underneath so that the holes can be put in a more secure position lower down the slate.

At the Ridge or Top Edge

As there are no nibs to consider, the top batten can be finished tight with the top edge, if required. The topper course of slates will need to be supported by an additional or a thicker batten placed behind the last course to prevent the tails lifting in high winds. In this case sufficient room must be allowed to accommodate this additional batten. Alternatively, the topper course can be bedded behind the heads of the toppers in mortar and nailed.

Gauge Adjustments

If your slates are pre-holed then you are likely to be stuck with a fixed gauge, but you should still find that there is some room to drop the gauges by a few millimetres, which is sometimes helpful if you want to adjust the gauges to come in with a full course at the ridge. If this is not possible, there is always the

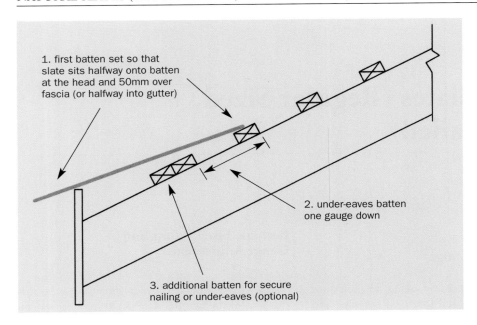

1. first batten set so that slate sits halfway onto batten at the head and 50mm over fascia (or halfway into gutter)

2. under-eaves batten one gauge down

3. additional batten for secure nailing or under-eaves (optional)

Batten positions at the eaves.

Typical ridge or top-edge finishes (thicker batten and bedded).

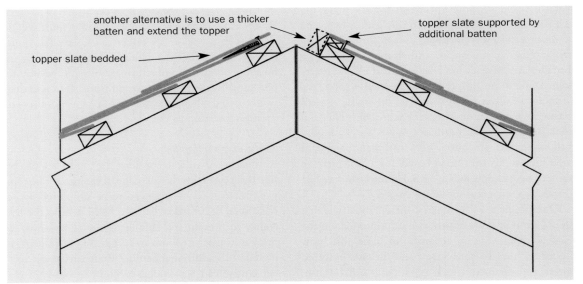

another alternative is to use a thicker batten and extend the topper

topper slate bedded

topper slate supported by additional batten

option of re-holing a proportion of the slates. Alternatively, you can stay with the gauge and just trim the last course of slates halfway on to the top batten.

Across the Roof

Traditionally, slate roofs were not normally marked out. The procedure was simply to lay the slates with a slight gap between them, then make any adjustments at the verges by cutting the second or the third slate in. However, slates may be marked out in much the same way as tiles, so cutting-in can sometimes be avoided and the perp lines will help to keep the slating straight and to half-bond.

A marking lath for slates of regular size is made as follows:

1. Add 3mm to the slate width and transfer sets of these marks to the marking batten. How many marks you put on is personal preference; you can mark every slate if like, but normally every third is sufficient.
2. Cross out the part that is spare, to avoid confusion later on.

Slates should retain a consistent gap, so, if you still cannot get the overhang you need by setting out, then be prepared to cut-in at the verge (second or third slate back) rather than try to open or close the slates.

GROUNDWORK

Grading

When you buy slates they tend to be 'pre-graded' by the quarry, but it is important to know what this really means. If the nominal thickness for a certain type of slate is, say, 4mm, the best slates (A grade) will be between 3 and 5mm thick. If you buy the cheaper slates (B grade) then the variance is greater. But, either way, you should still site-grade the slates because, if you do not, they will not sit properly, which not only looks awful but can leave the roof vulnerable to gale damage and driving rain. Grading has been neglected over the years, and perhaps more than any other skill in roofing because of the misconception that it is a luxury rather than a necessity. If you have a look at some old slate roofs you will find that most are laid almost perfectly flat with few if any gaps under the slates. Although the quality of the slates and the care exercised while laying them are definite factors, this flat, even finish was largely achieved by good grading. Compare this with some modern slated roofs that have many gaps, and the argument in favour of site grading is clear.

It is important to grade all the slates required before laying them so that the number of courses of each thickness can be established. The time lost in this grading will be more than recouped during the fixing stage. It is a bad habit to begin laying slates before they are all graded as this invariably leads to sections of the roof being made up of slates of varying thickness that do not sit well together. When you grade slates, try to feel the difference in weight rather than the thickness, you may make a few mistakes at the beginning but you will be surprised just how quickly you pick this up. Slates should be graded into a minimum of three thicknesses – thick, medium and thin. As apprentices we were always taught by our slating masters to grade into five thicknesses (thick, medium-thick, medium, medium-thin and thin), but how widespread this practice was (or still is) I am not sure.

Holing on Site (or in the Slater's Yard)

Traditionally, slates are holed and graded in the same operation on site or in the slate yard for individual roofs on a slater's bench. The bench will be set up to incorporate a bench/break iron, a holing machine and adequate space to stack slates ready for sorting and holing.

The holing points should be marked on the reverse side of the slate (known as its bed) at gauge + headlap + 6 to 12mm. The 6 to 12mm are needed so that the holes clear the head of the slate below when nailing.

When battens of smaller size were used it was always a good idea to set the holes just above the head of the slate, so 6mm clearance was often used. However, assuming that you are using the correct battens (50mm × 25mm) and using metric slates, then the norm now seems to be a clearance of 10mm. This makes the calculation easier and provides a well located hole for nailing.

An example of a holing point: 160mm gauge + 80mm headlap + 10mm clearance gives a holing point at 250mm; the holes should also be set 20 to 25mm in from the edges. (Note that, quite confusingly, the face of the slate is known traditionally as the 'back'.)

Once the holing point has been established, the holing machines can then be set to receive all the slates by adjusting the metal guide rails. The slate is holed from the bed to create a countersunk hole on the face, so that, when the slate is nailed, the head of the nail will sit in this hollow and does not stick above the line of the slate. It is important to keep the holes small so that the slate will not move about once nailed and is accurately positioned to avoid any re-holing. As each slate is holed, it is graded by thickness in readiness for loading and laying.

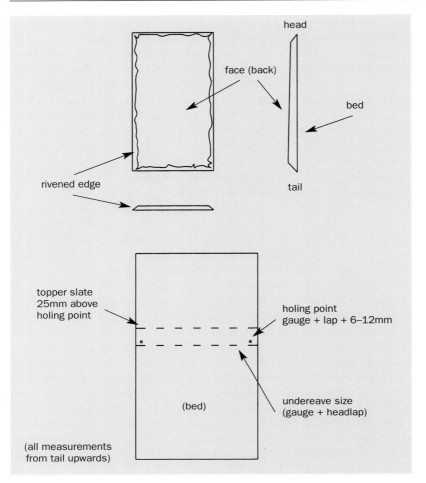

Holing points and other slate terminology.

head

face (back)

bed

rivened edge

tail

topper slate 25mm above holing point

holing point gauge + lap + 6–12mm

(bed)

undereave size (gauge + headlap)

(all measurements from tail upwards)

BELOW: Holing from the 'bed' creates a countersunk hole for the nail heads.

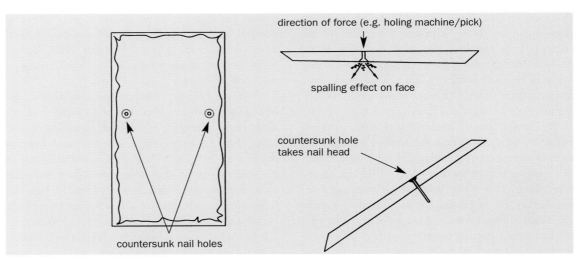

direction of force (e.g. holing machine/pick)

spalling effect on face

countersunk hole takes nail head

countersunk nail holes

Holing by hand with a sharpened pick or the spike of a slate knife should normally be reserved for repairs and small numbers of slates. For all but small quantities, holing by hand is more time-consuming, less accurate and less consistent than with a holing machine. There is also more spalling (the fragments of slate lost out of the countersunk hole) when holing by hand.

Cutting Techniques

General

Always mark and cut the slates from the bed (underside) of the slate. Cutting from the bed recreates the 'rivened' or 'chamfered' edge on the face of the slate. The only exception to this is when you are cutting mitred hips and valleys (these are advanced details, not covered here), in which the slates are cut from on the face.

Slate Knife

The basic technique is to keep the slate flat and close to the edge of the break iron and to apply long, steady strokes, letting the knife do the work – be smooth, do not hack at it. The motion should be similar to that of scissors going through cardboard. If you have a lot of slate to cut off, you can remove most

of this by picking a line of holes through it about 50mm from the cut line and knocking off the unwanted section. Then, trim off about 25 to 30mm at a time, leaving about 10 to 15mm for the final cut. Move the slate knife carefully and steadily down the line for the final cut.

Hand-Held Cutters

In my opinion, there are pros and cons associated with hand-held cutters. The pros are that they make less mess and may be quicker because you cut straight through the slate on the line you want. Another plus is that you can often use the off-cut part of the slate somewhere else (for instance, if you cut for a valley, the other part may go on the hips). The cons are that, once they start to deviate off line, it is sometimes difficult to get them back on to it, and they do not normally cope well with thicker slates.

Making the Fittings

During the grading and holing stage, slightly damaged slates should be kept to one side rather than be thrown away as they may be useful for making the 'fittings' (under-eaves, toppers and halves). Even the cheapest slates are still relatively expensive and so it makes sense to make use of the damaged ones first before cutting up the good ones. For

Using the spike for removing surplus slate.

Trimming to line with slate knife.

Under-eaves course.

First course of slates.

example, a slate with a broken bottom left-hand corner could be cut and trimmed down the centre and used at the right-hand verge and one with a broken top corner could be cut down for an under-eaves slate.

Verge Fittings (Half Slates and Slate-and-a-Half)

It is important to remember that half slates should be no less than 150mm at the verge and that the trimmed edges should be placed on the inside. For slates less than 300mm in width (for example, for a 250mm-wide slate the half would be only 125mm) you should use slates-and-a-half at the verge. You should find that they are readily available for new slates but are virtually unheard of in the reclaimed slate market, which is why you often see halves narrower than 150mm. Note that the nail holes nearest the verge will normally need to be moved in a little from the edge so that they are in line with the ends of the battens.

Under-Eaves and Topper Slates

The length of an under-eaves slate is always gauge + headlap, as measured up from the tail. For example, an under-eaves slate with a 260mm gauge and an 80mm headlap would be 260mm + 80mm = 340mm in length. Toppers should be cut 25mm above the nail holes.

Loading

The thickest slates should be loaded out at the lower parts of the roof as they are more durable, followed by those of medium thickness, with the thinnest slates used in the top few courses, to match how the roof will actually be laid. Never load out more than you expect to fix down in a day, especially if high winds, snow or ice are expected. Most right-handed slaters like to have the slates stacked with the bed (reverse side) facing them and the nail holes to the left, so that the slates can be picked up and placed more quickly.

FIXING DETAILS

Eaves

The eaves should be formed with one course of under-eaves slates laid at half-bond to the first course of slates. If you start with a full under-eave, then the first course will start with a slate-and-a-half or a half slate. If you start with half an under-eave, then your first course will start with a full slate. The top edge of the under-eaves should be laid halfway on to the batten as shown.

If the kick (the fascia board) at the eaves is too high and separation between the lower courses occurs then you may need to use longer nails. Alternatively, you could build up the battens as shown to support the slates.

Additional support battens to compensate for high fascia boards.

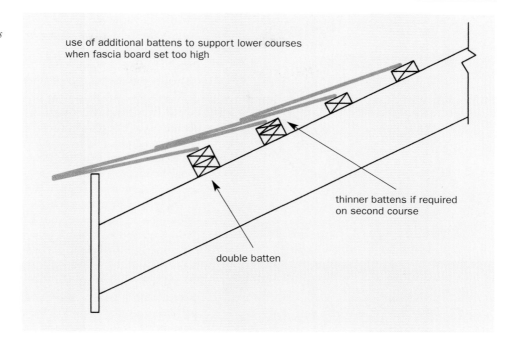

use of additional battens to support lower courses when fascia board set too high

thinner battens if required on second course

double batten

Verge

The procedure at the verge is to use full slates and halves or slates-and-a-half on every other course to break the bond. Slates are normally laid on to undercloak at 38 to 50mm, as with other materials, but they may also be bedded straight on to the verge if it is a masonry (such as brickwork or stone) finish. If this latter detail is used then the overhang tends to be brought in to just a few millimetres to protect the overhanging slate from the wind.

To point the verge, run the trowel at a slight angle underneath the slates to leave the edges clean.

The standard width and half slates (or slates-and-a-half) that make up the verge are never cut down, but the slates adjacent to them may be trimmed to fit if necessary.

Slating to verge and mortar finish.

Slating to General Areas (Main Roof)

All centre-nailed, natural slates should be fixed with two nails (normally of copper, unless otherwise stated) of 3.35mm diameter and sufficient length to penetrate at least 15mm into the batten. While it is obviously important to make sure that the nails are long enough, care should also be taken to ensure that the nails are not too long either, as this can lead to their going through the batten and puncturing the

underlay. For most mass-market, good quality, Spanish or Welsh slates, 30mm-nails should be fine, although longer ones may be needed for thicker slates. The slate supplier should be able to advise you on which nail size to use for the slates in question.

When you pick a slate up to lay it, it should be tapped lightly with a hammer to check for cracks or damage. If it 'rings' then it is in good condition, but if there is a dull sound coming from it then it is likely to be cracked, or, if you are using reclaimed slates, it could be soft or suffering from delamination (flaky and with a porous surface).

The general procedure is to set the slate so that it is halfway on to the batten and is running parallel to the top edge. Then, before you nail it, you should make a quick visual check to make sure that your nail hole does not fall in line with a knot in the batten (but, if it does, then make a new nail hole) and that there are no lumps or distortions in the slate that are likely to cause the next course above to rock (if there are, then put the slate to one side for later). If you do discard any bad slates look to trim them down or use them where they might not cause disruption. The next thing to do is to check that the slate is level with its neighbour with regard to thickness. If it is not, then find one that is and, if it is of the right thickness, then nail the slate in place, taking care to ensure that you have left a small gap between the slates.

At the top edge, mark the margin of the slate along the top course to keep the topper course straight. If you are bedding the toppers, use about half a trowelful of mortar per slate near the head and nail the topper in place, alternating between nailing it and knocking it down into the bed.

Open Valleys

(For valley board and lead-lining, *see* the open valleys section on plain tiles.) When cutting open valleys with slate they should normally be fixed dry without

TOP: *Slating to general areas.*

MIDDLE: *Marking a line for the toppers.*

BOTTOM: *Bedding and fixing the toppers.*

Marking slates to open valley.

Installing the first course.

Cut slate fixed in place.

mortar. The slates come into the valley and are cut to rake (angle) each side to leave a parallel channel of 125mm or more, depending on the width of lead used and the expected water content. Traditionally, open, lead-lined valleys were left wide enough to be walked up because they were always seen as access routes up and down the roof. If you have the choice, make yours wide enough to do this (that is, go for wider boards and lead) because it can make future roof inspection and maintenance much easier.

As regards the actual slating, the technique is to mark or strike a line on the lead and cut the slates to it. Although you mark initially on the face of the slate, this needs to be transferred to the bed for cutting.

The cut slates must be fixed twice. Note that it is quite acceptable to cut natural slates to a point in the valleys. The valley board can be used as a fixing point, provided, of course, that the nail is outside the valley lining.

It is a common misconception that you must use slates-and-a-half in open valleys. While it is true to say that they are handy for avoiding the very small cuts that are difficult to fix, they can actually cause sidelap problems on the course above when the cut does not carry far enough into the valley.

Bedded Ridge and Hip tiles

The procedure for bedding hip and ridge tiles has been covered extensively in the two previous chapters

Incorrect use of slates-and-a-half.

BELOW: Open valley in progress.

and so needs no repetition. The only real difference is that pointing to the side edges is required on tiles, but not necessarily on slates. If you look at some old slate roofs, you will notice that you cannot actually see any pointing at the sides. This is possible with slates because the ridge tile has been 'secret' or 'back' bedded on the inside edges and pressed right down on to the slate, thereby closing the gap that would normally be pointed. Now, of course, many of the techniques employed in roof tiling have crept into slating (which is regrettable and especially for traditionalists), so the convention now is to bed slate ridges and hip tiles a little higher and point them up.

The slates to the hips may be cut from the front, if you find this easier, as the edges are to be covered up anyway, but try to ensure that the cut line stays quite close to the hip and the cuts are securely fixed. Slates-and-a-half are useful when cutting up hips, but, because they can be quite expensive, they are rarely used for this type of detail.

Abutments

Slate abutments are weathered by using the same details as plain tiles using code 3 soakers and code 4 step flashings. The soaker length is technically worked out as gauge + lap + 25mm, with the width a minimum of 175mm (100mm on to slate + 75mm upstand). The bottom edge of the soaker should not be visible and is usually drawn back slightly from the tail of the slate, while the top edge may be nailed into the batten for security. In reality, because the soakers are drawn back slightly and can be nailed for slates, the 25mm added to form a 'nib' to hang on the batten is often discounted. If the slates have to be cut to fit, then the cut edge should go against the abutment.

Checking Reclaimed Slates

Good quality, second-hand slates are worth a great deal of money, especially the medium to larger sizes, so efficient salvaging is important and may be quite lucrative as well. When you are buying reclaimed slates it is not realistic to examine every one, but it is always wise to have a quick check through the batch in several places before you agree to the purchase. Try to avoid buying delaminated slates (with flaky surfaces) or slates that have been coated or with enlarged or damaged nail holes.

CHAPTER 9

Artificial Slates (Fibre-Cement)

Fibre-cement slates can normally be laid on roof pitches as low as 20 degrees (check conditions with individual manufacturers) right up to vertical cladding. The two most commonly used sizes in Britain are 600mm × 300mm and 500mm × 250mm, laid to a 100mm headlap. The gauge for fibre-cement slates is normally given in the manufacturer's information (in this case, 250mm and 200mm, respectively), but, if you need to work it out, the same formula is applied as for natural slates and plain tiles (that is, length – lap, divided by 2). It is important to establish the amount of headlap the slates have been holed for because this affects the batten gauge. Nails should be 30mm copper clout, unless otherwise specified. Disc rivets are also copper and are usually supplied in boxes of 1,000.

It is important to remember that the minimum batten size for fibre-cement slates is 50mm × 25mm.

Storing and Loading out

A chemical reaction known as efflorescence, causing white staining, can occur if the slates get wet when stacked tightly together. The main cause of this on site is through condensation in the packs, which are invariably shrink-wrapped in plastic. It is good practice to restack the slates in such a way that plenty of air can circulate around them and then to cover them with a tarpaulin. If the slates are to be used within a short time, then making a series of slits in the plastic wrapping may be acceptable. With this problem in mind, it is preferable to plan deliveries in stages to coincide with the use of the slates.

Never load out more than you expect to fix in a day, especially if high winds or snow are expected.

Most right-handed slaters like to have the slates stacked with the undersides of the slates facing them and the nail holes to the left so that the slates can be picked up and placed more quickly.

SETTING OUT

Batten Positions at the Eaves

There will need to be three thicknesses of slate at the eaves, and all the components that make this detail up should be available before the fixed points at the eaves can be established. The three thicknesses consist of the normal under-eaves and the first course arrangement found in natural slating, plus an additional 'dummy' eaves course. The under-eaves and dummy slates are cut from full slates. For 600mm × 300mm slates, the slates are cut across at gauge plus lap (for instance, 250mm + 100mm = 350mm) to provide an off-cut of 250mm for the dummy. The sole job of the dummy eaves is to provide support for the first line of rivets, which would simply drop out were it not there.

The positioning of the battens for the first course, under-eaves and dummy eaves will depend on the size of the slates and the specified headlap. Generally, the following rules apply:

- The top edge of the first course batten should be positioned at slate length + 25mm, measured from 50mm over the fascia (for instance, measure 50mm over and mark off at 625mm).
- The top edge of the under-eaves batten should be set one gauge down from the above (for instance, 250mm down).

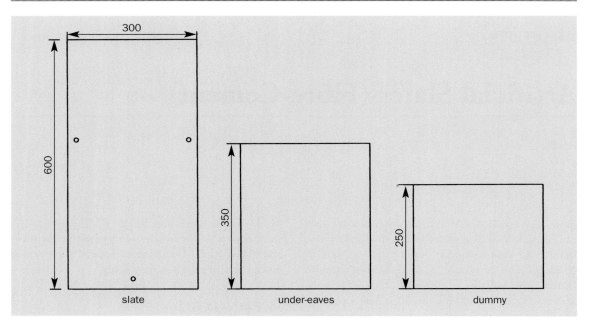

Under-eaves and dummy eaves cut from full slates.

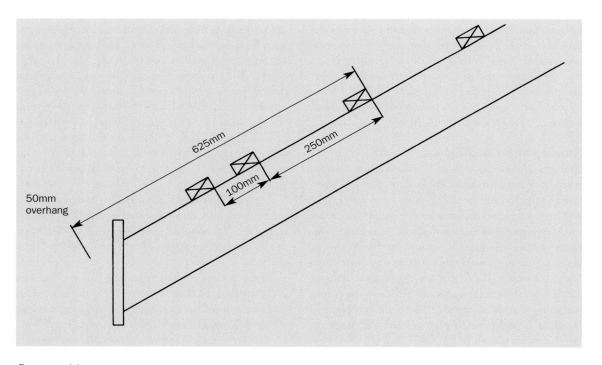

Batten positions at eaves.

- The top edge of the dummy eaves batten should be down from the above at a distance equal to the headlap (for instance, another 100mm down).

Fibre-cement slates are extremely fragile if not fully supported, so there should be little or no kick on the eaves and sprockets should be avoided. Lifting the tails up above the natural line of the slating causes weak points and a loss of support for the disc rivets in the lower courses. If you cannot reduce the height of the fascia board then the under-eaves battens should be increased in height to provide more lift and support to the affected area (*see* the picture on page 121).

General Battening and Slate Positioning

It is important that the batten gauges are correct and fixed to a struck line. Irregular gauges may cause loss of headlap as well as fixing problems, such as holes being in the wrong place and heads gradually falling off the support batten. Deviations, which are often associated with not using a line, can be transferred to the tail alignment of the slates, if the top edge is used as a parallel reference. Striking a line along the battens (halfway up) is a good way to keep the heads and therefore the tails of the slates straight and can speed up the fixing process, especially for beginners and inexperienced roofers.

Setting Out across the Roof (Striking Perp Lines)

Accurate positioning of the slates is a vital part of fibre-cement slating so correct and careful setting out is important. When marking across the roof, slate widths plus a 3 to 5mm gap should be used. The wider of the two will give you a little more room to slide the rivets up and down and tends to make the slating a little easier, in my opinion. If your tape has imperial measurements on it, a convenient cheat is to mark 300mm slates out at 12in intervals, with the half slate at 6in. This makes setting out very easy because you start at either verge with a full slate (for instance, 50mm over the verge, mark off 300mm), and from there mark 6, 12, 18, 24 and so on, on the imperial scale. This gives a consistent gap a shade under 5mm, which is perfect.

Striking perpendicular lines for the slates.

Transfer the marks to a marking batten, if you are comfortable doing that. With this particular material, my preference is to strike every slate, but you can do every third, if you prefer. Some roofers do not see the need to strike these slates at all, but it is normally beneficial to have at least some reference points. It is all down to personal preference and, provided the slating is straight and comes in properly at the verges, there is no hard and fast rule.

It is always better to try the roof through to see whether you can adjust your verge overhangs to fit the slates, but, if you cannot adjust the overhangs, all you need to do is to trim to width the slates one back from the finishing verge. Once you have decided on your overhang, mark the full and the half slates (or slates-and-a-half) widths on the starting verge and then apply the marks (slate widths + 3 to 5mm) to the bottom and the top course. Then strike lines between the corresponding points to ensure correct alignment.

CUTTING TECHNIQUES

Under-eaves slates, halves, slates-and-a-half and tops will all have to be cut unless the manufacturer can offer them preformed. It is highly desirable if you can get them, but check what premium (if any) you are paying for this service.

Slates can be cut by scribing and snapping over a straight edge or by 'nibbling' through with hand-held cutters.

MORTAR WORK

Mortar does not usually adhere well to fibre-cement slates without help, so it is recommended that a bonding agent be added to the mix. The manufacturers do not normally advise you on how much bonding agent to use because it depends on the type, but for standard PVA liquid adhesive (readily available from all DIY stores) I would recommend one 5ltr tin per mixer full of mortar.

You should also apply the bonding agent to the surfaces of the slates (and to ridge tiles, if applicable) and ensure that this is set before bedding takes place. I have also seen wire mesh glued to the slates (with PVA) to provide a key for mortar in some cases.

FIXING DETAILS

Basic Laying Procedure

All standard width slates should be twice nailed and riveted once at the tail. The head of the slate should sit halfway on to the battens. The nail holes should sit above the head of the course below by about 10mm, to provide a continuous fixing point just above the centre of the battens.

Fibre-cement slates are laid thus:

1. Insert rivets between slates (below the nails) during fixing.

TOP: Score the slate three or four times with the scribe.

MIDDLE: Snap over a clean straight edge.

BOTTOM: Cutting with 'hand-held' slate cutters.

TOP: Hooking the slate on to the rivet.

MIDDLE: Knocking down the rivet.

BOTTOM: Laying the dummy eaves and under-eaves.

2. Hook the slate above over the rivet.
3. Knock the rivet down.
4. Move the slate into position and nail it.

Accurate and consistent positioning of the rivet is important for speed of fixing. Ideally, it should be set down from the head of the slate it rests on at a distance of 25mm less than the headlap (for example, 75mm down for a 100mm headlap). If you can achieve this consistently, then the slates will be at the correct height each time and so any adjustments should be minor. It is now possible to find specially designed rivet guides, which set the rivet at the perfect height every time and, although I have not used one myself, there is evidence to suggest that they can save on fixing times, especially on larger roofs.

Eaves
Begin by nailing the dummy eaves in place. You may need to re-hole these to ensure a secure fixing because the existing nail holes are quite near the top of the slate and are inclined to break off now and again. Fix the under-eaves to the marks, placing a rivet between each one at approximately 25mm up from the tail. Note how the nail holes in the under-eaves are set down from the head by 100mm (that is, a distance equal to the headlap). This prevents the tail of the slate from tipping up and putting downwards pressure on the tail of the slate and therefore on the rivets.

Verges
Wet-fix verges are constructed in the standard way by nailing or bedding undercloak to the wall or bargeboard at the desired overhang (preferably 38 to 50mm), and then bedding and pointing the slate on to it. The slates may actually be cut in half lengthways and used as undercloak (laid the good side down) to form an effective finish.

Verges are normally formed by using standard width slates and slates-and-a-half on every other

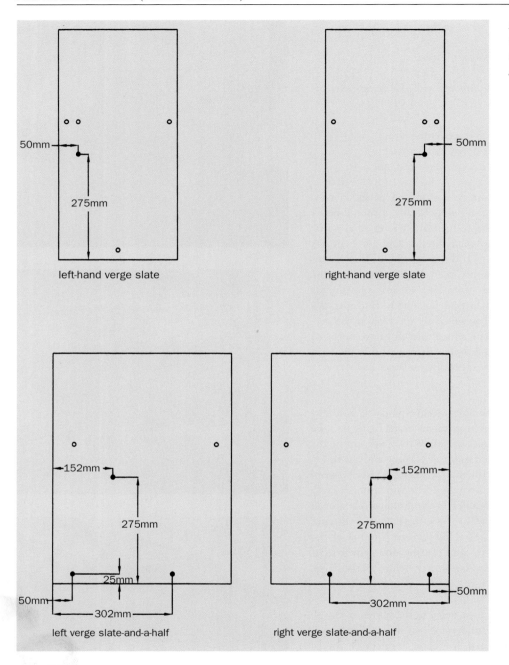

Re-holing of verge slates with slates-and-a-half.

left-hand verge slate

right-hand verge slate

left verge slate-and-a-half

right verge slate-and-a-half

course. New nail holes and rivet holes will have to be formed in the verge slates. Holes should be formed using a 3mm masonry drill bit to the positions shown (rivet holes in solid black).

If you cannot get slates-and-a-half then you may need to buy double slates and cut them down to size. Where this applies, the cut edge always goes on the inside. The picture (above) shows where the two

TOP: *Starting off at the verge.*

MIDDLE: *Positioning the first verge slate.*

BOTTOM: *Fixing the first verge slate and inserting rivet.*

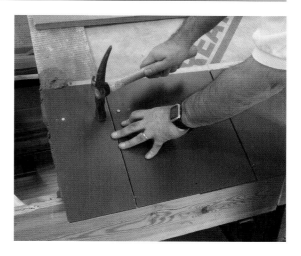

main nail holes need to be positioned, but an additional one will also have to be formed (in situ) because all slates-and-a-half should be fixed with three nails. Normally, the best place for the third hole is about 100mm in from the verge.

The standard procedure for installing a standard verge detail is:

1. The verge normally starts with half an under-eave or a slate-and-a-half under-eave cut down to size; remember to insert the rivet.
2. Next, locate the first verge slate. Position a rivet in the hole just below the nail holes and hold it between your fingers to prevent it from falling out while you hook the slate over the rivet at the eaves.
3. Once the slate in is place, knock the bottom rivet down and nail the slate, insert another rivet about 75mm below the nail hole and lay two or three more slates to prepare for the next course.
4. From here it is just a case of fixing slates and slates-and-a-half in alternate courses and slating away from the verge as necessary; the important thing to remember is to install all the rivets in the right holes, although drilling all the holes first does help in this respect because what you need to do becomes much more obvious.

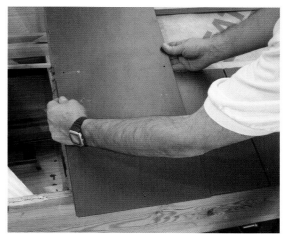

Slates-and-a-half or doubles are expensive, so some jobs are done with half slates on the verges. If you score and snap full slates exactly down the middle you will find that you can use both halves at the verges (cut edges to the inside). Bear in mind that most manufacturers recommend slates-and-a-half so, if you choose to go with half slates, you are advised to check with the manufacturer to see how this may or may not affect your warranty.

ABOVE: *Slating to verge in progress.*

TOP LEFT: *Slating away from the verge.*

LEFT: *Top courses trimmed halfway on to batten.*

Short Courses

At the Ridge and Top Edges

Because these types of slate are fixed gauge, short courses are common and usually unavoidable. The last full course should be trimmed halfway on to the top batten and a topper course cut to maintain the slate margins and provide sufficient cover for the ridge tiles.

At Eaves

Depending on regional practice or personal preference, the short course can also be positioned at the eaves. To form a short course in this way, the first fixed points at the eaves are set as normal, but the rest of the gauges are set down from the top edge. This results in a reduced gauge between the top edge of the first full course and the second

*Re-holing when
using half slates.*

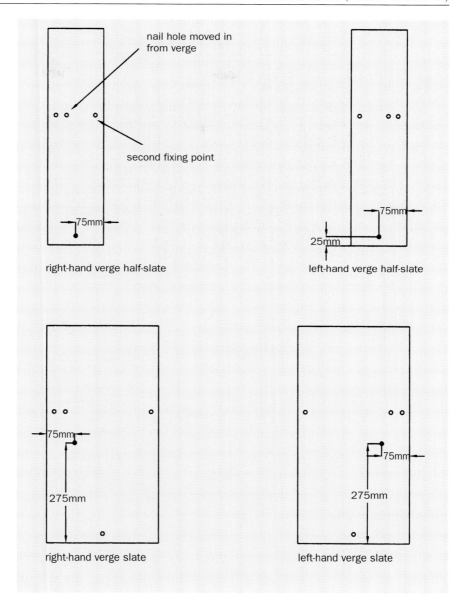

nail hole moved in
from verge

second fixing point

75mm

right-hand verge half-slate

75mm

25mm

left-hand verge half-slate

75mm

275mm

right-hand verge slate

75mm

275mm

left-hand verge slate

course. The short course is then created by allowing the slate on the second course to overlap the one below by an increased headlap and is fixed by repositioning the nail holes. The benefits of this are that there is no cutting (apart from a standard topper) and the short course is arguably less obtrusive than at the top edge.

Abutments

Slates should be cut as closely as possible to the sides of chimneys and other abutments to provide as much lap and support as possible to the flashings. The cut edge of the slate should always be placed next to the wall and slates-and-a-half or doubles used to avoid small pieces where necessary. The usual flashing

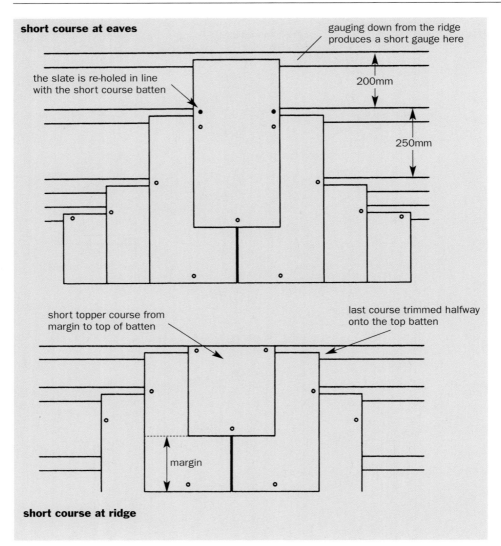

short course at eaves

gauging down from the ridge
produces a short gauge here

the slate is re-holed in line
with the short course batten

200mm

250mm

short topper course from
margin to top of batten

last course trimmed halfway
onto the top batten

margin

short course at ridge

*Short courses
at eaves and
ridge.*

detail is a step flashing over soakers, the same as for natural slates and plain tiles.

Ridges

Proprietary fibre-cement ridge coverings are fixed dry on to the slates with wood screws and made watertight with sealing washers (both supplied with the ridge tiles) and mastic. The ridge tiles lap over one another like a cap ridge and are sealed between the joints with a bead of mastic. The fixings are then located into the battens through site-drilled holes (usually one on each side of the cap and one on each side at mid-distance).

Hips

Hips are finished in the same way as the ridge tiles but with a shallower unit designed to minimize the sweep at the three-way intersection. The intersection should be covered with a lead saddle, which can be held in place by passing through the corresponding drive screws.

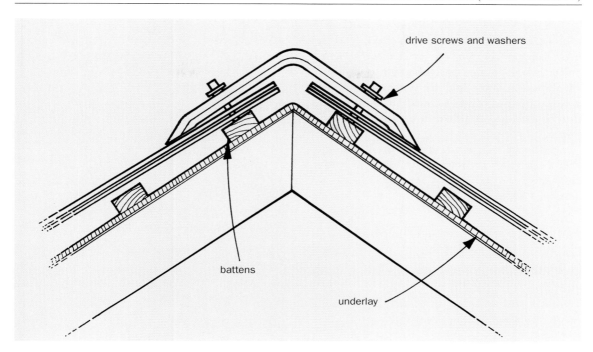

ABOVE: Fibre-cement ridge tiles.

RIGHT: Marking slates in the valley.

Open Valleys

Fibre-cement slates should never be cut to a point in the valleys, and doubles may be used to avoid this problem. The double slates are supplied blank without nail holes or rivets to give maximum flexibility in a variety of situations. This does mean, of course, that there will be some holing for nails and rivets to be done. Positioning new nail holes is fairly straightforward. At least two nail holes should be made at gauge + headlap + 10mm (as measured up from the tail of the slate), with special consideration being given to the hole nearest the valley to ensure that it is over a secure fixing point.

Accurately positioning new rivet holes is rather trickier. You will need one rivet hole near the tail of each cut slate (normally 25mm up, and half the width of the tail across) and a second one at gauge + 25mm up, and half the distance of the tail width across for the course above.

If all this appears complicated do not worry, there is no need to be too obsessed with perfect positioning. The important thing is to make sure that there is a rivet hole in approximately the right place for the tail of the next course, and that you insert a rivet into it before you nail the slate down. The next hole can then be lined up with the rivet in both directions as shown.

Check after each course that each tail is secured with a rivet and that there are at least two nails in each slate.

RIGHT: Marking the position of the next rivet hole (across).

BELOW LEFT: Marking the position of next rivet hole (up).

BELOW RIGHT: Valley in progress, each tail riveted.

CHAPTER 10

Basic Flashings

Lead work is a skill all on its own and so describing how to form and install all these flashings is outside the scope of this book. To get the flashings right is essential because they keep the junctions watertight, so I would suggest that anything more complicated than installing soakers, simple saddles or pipe flashings should really be done by an experienced roofer, plumber or lead worker. However, I have included this short chapter to give the reader some awareness of basic flashings.

GENERAL

Flashings are impervious (watertight) sheets of lead, copper, zinc, rigid bitumen sheet, tin, plastic or aluminium, shaped and installed at roof junctions to prevent the penetration of rain and snow. The most commonly used material is sheet lead, and it will be on this material that this chapter will mainly concentrate.

Proprietary flashings (for example, roof window flashings) should not be modified, cut nor used in any way that might conflict with the manufacturer's instructions, since there could be a risk of leaks, and the conditions of any guarantee or warranty would be broken.

Lead Sizes and Codes

Sheet lead is sold in rolls from 150mm wide and in lengths from 3m upwards. The most common widths used in slating and tiling are 150, 225, 300, 375 and 450mm. The code of the lead is an indication of its thickness (and therefore weight). This will be shown by a strip of coloured tape stuck to the roll. The fol-

lowing codes are the ones most commonly used in slating and tiling:

Code 3 (green; 1.32mm minimum thickness) for soakers and other work not directly exposed to the weather. This is the thinnest and lightest of the codes that we use, it needs to be thin because bulky soakers would lift the slate or tile; it is the lightest because weight is not important for soakers since there is no exposure to wind uplift.

Code 4 (blue; 1.80mm minimum thickness) for all flashings such as saddles and step flashings; these flashings are exposed to the weather and so have to be more durable and heavier to resist the elements.

Code 5 (red; 2.24mm minimum thickness) used where there is expected to be a high concentration of water, as in the valleys and box gutters.

Colour-coded lead roll.

Step flashing over soakers.

Anti-patination oil should be applied with a cloth to prevent weeping white stains (a natural discharge from the lead when exposed) wherever it is likely to run on to the tiles or slates. This should be done as soon as the new lead is installed.

DETAILS

Abutments

At side abutments there are three types of flashing: soakers, step flashings and secret gutters.

Step Flashings and Soakers

All double-lap materials such as plain tiles, fibre-cement slates and natural slates use soakers and step flashing. The soakers are cut to size by using the formula:

length: gauge + headlap + 25mm; width: 175mm (unless otherwise stated; 100mm on to the slate or tile and 75mm upstand)

Step flashings for double-lap materials such as slates and plain tiles are usually cut from 150mm code 4 lead. The flashing is cut so that 25mm is turned into the brickwork and a 'water line' of 65mm is retained, below which the lead should not be cut. The step flashing is installed over the soakers to form a water-tight junction in lengths of no more than 1.5m, with minimal overlaps of 150mm. The flashing is secured by using lead wedges and a pointing material, usually mortar, although mastic is actually preferable as it copes better with the expansion and contraction of the lead as the temperature varies.

Step and cover flashing for interlocking tiles.

Step and Cover Flashings

Step flashings for interlocking tiles require the lead to be wider so that it extends on to the tiles and over the first roll. Soakers are unsuitable and unnecessary for this type of work. Widths of 300 to 375mm are normally used, depending on the required width.

Top Edges

Flashings under windows, at the top edges of porches and integral garages, for example, should be fixed in 1.5m lengths with 150mm overlap at the side. The depth of flashing and therefore the roll width is determined by the height of the relevant brickwork course (minimal upstand of 75mm) + 25mm for the turn into the joints + enough coverage on to the top course to maintain the minimum headlap. Often straps and/or folds are used for greater resistance to wind uplift.

Valleys

Open valleys use code 4 or 5 lead in maximum lengths of 1.5m with 150mm minimal laps. The lead is 'welted' or folded back at the side edges to prevent any penetrating rain from entering the roof. The most commonly used roll widths for valleys are normally 375 or 450mm. Interlocking tiles will need an undercloak at the sides for bedding mortar on to lead valleys, otherwise the mortar will crack away as the lead expands and contracts.

Top edge abutment flashings.

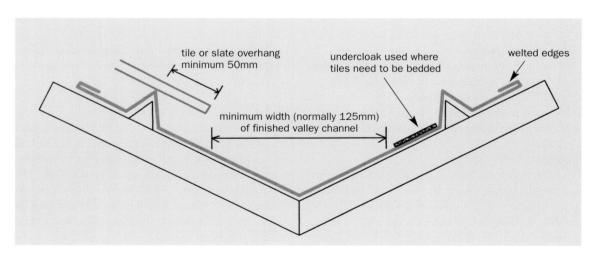

tile or slate overhang
minimum 50mm

undercloak used where
tiles need to be bedded

welted edges

minimum width (normally 125mm)
of finished valley channel

Lead-lined valley.

Soil and Vent Pipes

Lead slates for soil and vent pipes are usually made from code 4 lead. A size of 400mm × 400mm is usually adequate and 150mm is recommended as the minimal upstand and for all sidelaps. When installing a lead slate it is important to make sure that all the lead underneath the tile or slate courses is supported so that it cannot sag. Welting (folding) the back and concealed side edges by about 25mm gives extra protection against driving rain. Once the tiles have been cut and the lead slate installed, a collar should be fitted (often with a mastic bead first) over the pipe to seal the joint.

Saddles

Saddles are sections of lead sheet used to weather junctions like the tops of valleys, where the ridge comes into a wall, for instance. Simple saddles are usually formed from a single piece of lead and simply bossed or dressed into shape, but more complicated ones may need to be lead-welded.

Typical lead slate.

CHAPTER 11

Repairs and Maintenance

This chapter deals with how to spot the sources of leaks and common defects and also how to replace defective slates and tiles. It also explains how repointing should be carried out and, where this is not appropriate, how to strip, clean and reapply fresh mortar.

But, an important reminder: if you intend to go on to a roof make sure that you take all the relevant safety precautions described in the introduction, and, wherever possible, work with at least one other person who can remain mostly at ground level.

ROOF DEFECTS

Detecting Leaks

Some are obvious, but others are less so, and often a process of elimination is needed. When dealing with water ingress the leak may have started in a completely different place from where it shows up. When faced with a roof leak there are a few tips to help in finding the source:

- Identify where the leak is from inside the house.
- Step outside and look for any obvious signs, such as missing slates or tiles, especially above or in the valleys and missing flashings, for example. If you possess a pair of binoculars, these could be very useful.
- Look inside the loft space, if possible, to try and trace the leak to the source; the rafter should be damp down from where water has entered but dry above this point.
- If you suspect that the leak is in the valley, check for splits in the liner.

- Check that gutters are clear of debris and vegetation (especially at the foot of valleys), as water can back up under tiles or slates if it cannot get away.

Leaks may be very serious and costly if not traced and repaired in time. Long-term leaks can cause wet rot and irreparable damage to ceilings and walls. If the leak appears only very occasionally or during periods when heavy rain is accompanied by strong winds, this can be more difficult to detect and cure because the point of ingress may be much less obvious. Check around any pipes that may penetrate the roof to make sure that the collars are sealed, check that tiles or slates are not kicking up and that there are no obvious signs that mortar has fallen out.

Condensation

Damp patches and mould on the ceiling are assumed by most homeowners to indicate a roof leak, but it is often a condensation problem. Introducing ventilation products such as tile or slate vents, over-fascia vents and ridge vents should get rid of vapour-laden air before it can settle. If the damp is occurring above a condensation 'hot-spot', such as a bathroom or utility room, then a special tile or slate vent can be introduced or an extractor may help to combat the problem. In modern construction it is increasingly common to see 'breather' underlay applied to new roofs and re-roofs as an alternative to traditional venting methods.

Frost Damage

To varying degrees, all slates and tiles absorb some water. When this freezes the resulting expansion over

Delaminated tiles caused by years of freezing and thawing.

thousands of cycles can eventually cause cracks and delamination. This is perhaps most noticeable in clay tiles and slates and is found especially in wet areas, such as the eaves and the valleys, and especially on north-facing elevations of the roof.

Thermal Movement

Roofs, like the rest of the building, 'flex' when the weather conditions change. Some cracking of mortar can occur when the roof expands and contracts. This is not necessarily anything to worry about, but the situation should be monitored and, if the condition worsens, then remedial work may be necessary.

REPLACING SLATES AND TILES

Slates

Slate roofs are often stripped and recovered well before the slates perish. Usually the nails and battens that hold the slates deteriorate to such an extent that the weight of the slates becomes too much and they begin to slip out of position. The corrosion of slate nails leading to this problem is known as 'nail sickness' and, while in its early stages the roof may be repairable, the only real long-term solution is to strip the roof and re-slate it with new underlay, battens and nails.

145

Slate ripper position behind nail.

Slate ripper position in front of nail.

Repairing Slates

To remove a broken slate it is first necessary to remove the nails with a slate ripper. The nails may be forced out upwards by positioning the ripper in front of the nail, downwards by positioning behind the nails or by using a combination of the two. I have marked the nail positions and the outline of the slate to be ripped out to show these positions, because, once the ripper is fed under the slate, you would not be able to see them.

The most common method of removing a slate is to get behind the nails and rip it out, especially on older roofs where the nails have corroded. First, take the slate ripper and feed it underneath the slate until you can feel the hook locate behind either nail you

want to rip out. The nail can then be ripped out by hitting down on the handle of the slate ripper with a hammer or by sliding the ripper up slightly and yanking down hard and fast on the nail. Either way, it may take several strikes or yanks to get the nail out, depending on what condition the nails are in. Feel inside with your fingers to make sure that you have cleared all parts of the nail from the batten. If there is any part of a nail stuck, clear it with the ripper or a pair of pincers or pliers.

Once you are happy that the batten is clear, cut a thin strip of copper or lead to form a strap or 'tingle', as it is also known. Lead is perhaps the most commonly used because it is a material that most roofers routinely carry on their vans, but it is quite soft in comparison with copper and this can mean that the straps bend back over time, especially if the slates are heavy or are subjected to sliding snow and ice. The tingle should be about 20mm wide and the length should be equal to the headlap plus about 50mm. Nail the tingle between the seams of the slates and into the batten.

Sometimes, when you try to slide the replacement slate back in you may have difficulty getting the head of it on to the batten. To get round this you need to lift the head, and one way to do this is to put a nail on either side of the slate and press down on the tail while you roll the slate up into place. Once the replacement slate is installed, bend the tingle up to complete the repair.

When repairing a patch of slates try to use as few straps as possible. The recognized procedure is to strip the slates in a triangle so that, when they are replaced, they can be nailed back into place with just the last one relying on a strap. This is especially useful when stripping out and replacing long sections along the eaves. You will be able to get at only one of the nail holes of the slates at the outer edges of the triangle, so, to stop it swinging, you will need to nail it twice on the same side of the slate ('wing' nailing). When you do this, you must make sure that the second nail hole is at least 75mm away from the centre of the slate.

An alternative to wing nailing is to hang the side of the slate that you cannot get to, on a nail. This is simply a matter of forming a new hole just above the line of the batten, popping a nail in and sliding the slate into place. The exposed side of the slate is then nailed as normal.

It is also acceptable to use steel slate hooks for repairs and there are also several proprietary slate repair products on the market today. Alternatively, copper wire can be used (if you are using wire, twist a loop into one end to take the nail). Also, it is a good idea to create a 'home' for the wire by inserting a small nick into the bottom edge of the slate first.

TOP: Slate ripper fed in behind nail.

BELOW: Ripping out the nails.

Nailing the tingle in position.

Slide the slate into position (nails used as a pivot to lift the head).

Tingle turned up to complete the repair.

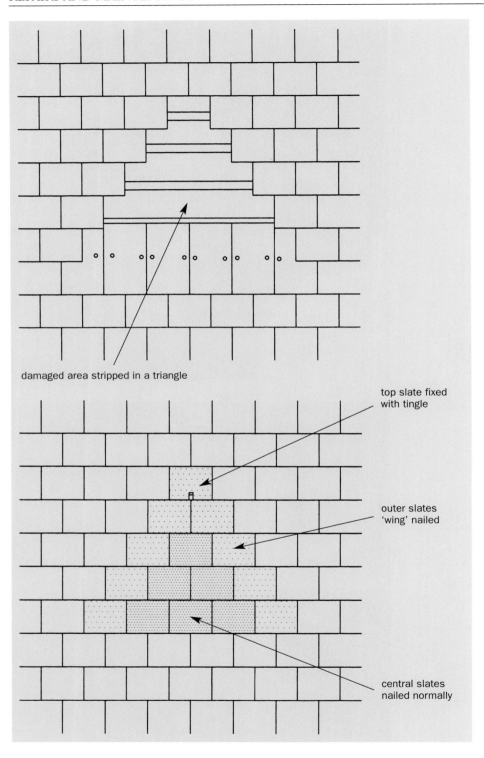

An area of slates stripped and repaired with minimal straps.

damaged area stripped in a triangle

top slate fixed with tingle

outer slates 'wing' nailed

central slates nailed normally

150

REPLACING TILES

Replacing tiles is normally much easier than replacing slates; you can, for example, take a square of tiles out rather than a triangle and do not need special ripping tools or tingles. Whatever types of tile you are replacing, always try to strip them from the highest point. You should find that, on most old roofs, not all the tiles are nailed, so you can normally push the tiles up (especially interlocking tiles) or lift them to expose the ones you want to take out. When you come to replace the tiles, simply nail them back to the same specification as the roof (or higher) and slide or lower the tiles back down to complete the repair.

RE-POINTING AND REPLACING MORTAR WORK

Re-Bedding

Clean off all old mortar before re-bedding. Use a hand brush to remove loose mortar and dampen the surface to remove dust and prevent premature drying out. Always bed and point on the same day, this ensures that the mortar sets 'as one', not in separate sections. If this cannot be done for any reason, then the bed must be cut well back, roughed up (for instance, marked in a criss-cross pattern with a trowel) to provide a key and then dampened before pointing.

Push or lift tiles up and strip out those to be replaced.

Replace tiles.

Lower the tiles back down into position.

Re-Pointing

If you are just re-pointing, hack and scrape out as much of the old, loose mortar as possible and remove any dust and debris with a hand brush. Always try to dampen the surface where the mortar will key into; one of the best methods of applying water is with the hand brush dipped in clean water.

152

Appendix: Estimating Materials

INDIVIDUAL ROOF AREAS

For standard roof formations there are only four basic shapes: the rectangle, triangle, parallelogram and trapezium.

square or rectangle = eaves length × rafter length
example: lean-to roof with 3m eaves length × 2.5m rafter = 7.5sq.m

triangle = eaves or ridge length × common rafter length, divided by 2
example: hip end with 5m eaves × 4m rafter = 20 divided by 2 = 10sq.m
parallelogram: as rectangle
example: hip to valley section of roof with eaves 4.5m × 3m rafter = 13.5sq.m
trapezium = [eaves length + ridge length] divided by 2 × rafter length

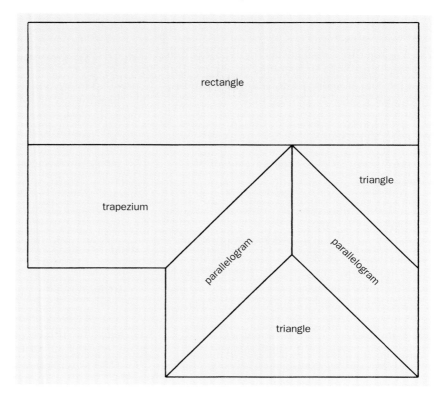

Standard roof areas.

example: hip to verge section with eaves 5m, ridge 2m and rafter 3m = 3.5 (7m divided by 2) × 3 = 10.5sq.m

NUMBER OF COURSES UP AND ACROSS THE ROOF

Other examples follow on how to estimate the quantities of tiles and slates required for any given area, but the most accurate way to estimate the slate or tile quantities is to multiply the number of tiles across the roof by the number of courses up the roof, as shown here.

up the roof = rafter length in metres divided by slate or tile gauge in metres
example: 5m divided by 0.345m (345mm) = 14.49 (15 courses)
across the roof = eaves length divided by covering width of the slate or tile
example: 6m divided by 0.300m (300mm) = 20 tiles across (in practice, this might be rounded up to 21 to allow for verge overhangs)
so, for this roof elevation we would need a total of 315 tiles (15 × 21)
ridge or hip tiles = total hip and/or ridge length (in metres) divided by length of tile (in metres)
example: 20m of combined hip lengths divided by 0.450m (450mm) = 45 ridge tiles

PLAIN TILES

standard tiles = area × 61 for pitched roofs (53 for vertical)
example: 13.5sq.m × 61 = 823.5 (824 tiles)
hip and valley tile fittings = 1 per course (multiply rafter length by 10)
example: 3.5m rafter × 10 = 35 fittings per hip or valley
under eaves/tops = eaves or ridge length divided by 165mm (tile width)
example: 4m eaves divided by 0.165m (165mm) = 25 under-eave tiles
tile-and-a-half = 1 per every second course at verges, abutments, open valleys, bonnets and concrete valley tiles (multiply rafter length by 5)

example: 3m rafter × 5 = 15 tiles-and-a-half each side of the roof

INTERLOCKING TILES

The approximate quantity may be found by multiplying the area by the number of tiles per square metre (check manufacturer information for tile types, but this is typically 9.7, say 10 per sq.m for the most common concrete interlocking roof tiles)
example: 40sq.m × 10 = 400 tiles

SLATES

standard slates = area multiplied by slates per square metre (check supplier information)
example: 40sq.m × 18 = 720 slates
slates-and-a-half = 1 per every other course at verges, abutments and valleys
example: 30 courses = 15 slates-and-a-half each side of the roof
under-eaves = eaves length divided by slate width
example: 6m eaves divided by 0.250m (250mm) = 24 under-eave slates

FELT OR UNDERLAY

area divided by net coverage of one roll (check manufacturer information)
example: 50sq.m divided by 12 = 4.17, say 5 rolls
note that you will normally need extra underlay for hips and valleys, so add the total length of hips and valleys together and divide this by the length of one roll
example: 26m of hip and valley, divided by 15m equals 1.73 (2 extra rolls)

BATTENS (LATHS)

total number of slates or tiles multiplied by the covering width of the slate or tile
example: 187 tiles × 0.30m (300mm) = 56.1, say 56m of batten, or divide the area by the batten gauge (in metres)
example: 45sq.m divided by 0.345m (345mm) = 130.4, say 130m of batten

Glossary

Abutments   where a roof meets the side of a wall, dormer or chimney

Apex   the highest point of the roof where the two slopes meet (*see* Ridge)

Arris hips   hip tile normally ordered to match the roof pitch when using plain tiles

Bargeboard   boards fixed to the underside of the verge at the gable ends

Batten gauge   or just gauge; the measurement for the batten centres (normally measured top edge to top edge)

Block end ridge   ridge tile with one end filled (often used with cloaked verge tiles)

Bonnet hips   hip tile used in plain tiling with raised edge for pointing

Cloaked verge   special tiles designed to turn down at the verge as an alternative to using mortar

Course   row of tiles or slates going across a roof

Dentil slips   small, rectangular sections of concrete or clay set into the 'pan' of a tile under a bedded ridge or hip tiles

Eaves   draining edges of a roof (the part of the roof above the gutter)

Eaves fillers   plastic sections (individual or in 1m combs) fixed on top of a fascia board to prevent birds and vermin from entering a roof

Fascia board   timber or PVC board found at the eaves (behind the guttering)

Finial   decorative end ridge tile with vertical feature (for instance, fleur-de-lis)

Fixed gauge   tiles and slates designed to be laid at a fixed or tightly governed batten gauge

Flashings   impervious strips fixed at junctions to make them weather-tight; lead is normally used for this purpose but other materials are also available

Half-bond   (also known as broken bond)   when tiles or slates are laid halfway across the course below

Headlap   distance by which a course of slates or tiles overlaps the slate or tile below

Hips   where two sloping roofs meet at an external corner of a house

Gauge   *see* Batten gauge

Left-hand-verge tiles   specially fitting tiles designed to finish off the left-hand side of tiling so that it is in keeping with the rest of the roof (for instance, double roll pan tiles)

Linear cover (also known as effective width) the visible width of a tile or slate once laid on a roof

Margin length of tile or slate left visible once it has been laid (equal to the batten gauge)

Mitre close, accurate cutting of materials at a junction

Overhang distance that the undercloak extends over the verge or the distance by which tiles or slates extend into a gutter

Pitch angle of the roof slope as measured from the horizontal

Ridge line running along the apex of a roof

Saddle flashing that covers a junction between two or more roof slopes

Sidelap distance by which one tile or slate is offset from the edge of the one below

Soakers small sections of watertight material (usually lead) used with slates and plain tiles, typically underneath a step flashing at abutments

Soffit area underneath the eaves between the underside of the fascia board and the wall

Sprocket shallow section at the eaves normally found on very steep roofs (such as steeples), designed to slow rainwater down before it reaches a gutter

Undercloak sections of slate/tile/fibre-cement strip used at a verge to provide a bedding key for the mortar at overhangs

Valleys line between two roof slopes at an internal corner of a house

Variable gauge tiles where the batten gauge can be adjusted (that is, reduced) to fit the rafter length

Verge outer edges of a roof area above the gable ends

Winchester cut decorative gable-end finish, normally done in plain tiles

Useful Contacts

MATERIALS

The National Federation of Roofing Contractors web site brings together a host of roofing-related topics. This particular link is to the materials page where many of the industry's leading manufacturers and suppliers are listed: www.nfrc.co.uk/Materials.aspx

LEADWORK

The Lead Sheet Association (01892 822773): www.leadsheetassociation.org.uk

HEALTH AND SAFETY

Health and Safety Executive (publications: 01787 881165; information: 0845 345 0055): www.hse.gov.uk

BRITISH STANDARDS INSTITUTION

Telephone: 020 8996 9001; email: orders@bsi-global.com; www.bsi-uk.com/StandardsAndPubs/index.xalter

ROOFING TRAINING

Probably the best place to start looking for training is through the Regional Roof Training Groups (RRTG); this link will take you to the central page: www.roofconsult.co.uk/training/rrtg.htm

The Construction Industry Training Board (CITB; 01485 577577) has recently been renamed Construction Skills, but at the time of writing (late 2007) this link was still live; the website has information on training, apprenticeships and many other matters related to construction on a national level: www.citb.co.uk/traininglearning/The Sandtoft Training and Assessment Centre, where most of the pictures shown in this book were taken, specializes in helping existing roofers to get their qualifications on site or through a practical test in the centre (01427 781252): www.sandtoft.co.uk/tiles/technical-support/training-cpd/training

Index